JESUS • Fathered by no man • Teacher to
all men • Gentle revolutionary proclaiming
love • Worker of miracles • Prophesier of
His own death • Executed by the Romans
• He came back from the dead
Who was He?
**"I am the way," He said, "no one can
come to God but by me."**
This is the true story of the life of Jesus
Christ.

Here is the fifth in the unique series
that brings all of the excitement, drama and
color of the Bible in words and pictures from
the world's greatest, truest Book!

The Picture Bible for All Ages

VOLUME 5

MATTHEW—JOHN

Script by Iva Hoth

Illustrations by Andre Le Blanc

Bible Editor, C. Elvan Olmstead, Ph.D.

David C. Cook Publishing Co.

850 NORTH GROVE AVENUE • ELGIN, IL 60120

In Canada: David C. Cook Publishing (Canada) Ltd., Weston, Ontario M9L 1T4

JESUS
First printing, June 1973
Second printing, September 1973
Third printing, October 1973
© 1973 David C. Cook Publishing Co., Elgin, IL 60120
All Rights Reserved. This book, or parts thereof,
may not be reproduced in any form without permission
of the publisher, except by a reviewer who wishes
to quote brief passages in connection with a review
in a magazine or newspaper.
Published by David C. Cook Publishing Co.
Printed in United States of America by Offset Paperbacks.
Library of Congress Catalog Card Number: 73-78172
ISBN: 0-912692-17-0

ILLUSTRATED STORIES

JESUS

> I am come that they
> might have life,
> and that they might
> have it more abundantly.
> I am the good shepherd:
> the good shepherd giveth
> his life
> for the sheep.
>
> JOHN 10: 10, 11

The Life of Jesus

FROM MATTHEW, MARK, LUKE, AND JOHN

THE FIRST FOUR BOOKS OF THE NEW TESTAMENT ARE CALLED THE GOSPELS, WHICH MEANS "GOOD NEWS"--ABOUT JESUS: HIS LIFE, TEACHINGS, DEATH, AND RESURRECTION. BECAUSE THE BOOKS ARE ALIKE IN MANY WAYS, THE FACTS HAVE BEEN COMBINED HERE TO TELL ONE STORY.

TO EVERYONE, JESUS SAYS-- I AM THE WAY... NO ONE CAN COME TO GOD BUT BY ME.

FOR ALMOST SIXTY YEARS PALESTINE, THE HOME OF THE JEWS, HAS BEEN RULED BY THE MIGHTY ROMAN EMPIRE. TO MAINTAIN THEIR CONTROL, THE ROMANS APPOINTED HEROD, A CLEVER BUT CRUEL MAN, TO RULE THE LAND. THE JEWS HATE HIM-- AND THE ROMAN OFFICIALS WHO COME TO HIS COURT. THE TIME IS NOW 6 B.C....

HERE, OLD MAN, CARRY THIS FOR ME.

THAT CHEST IS TOO HEAVY FOR SUCH AN OLD MAN.

THE ROMANS DON'T CARE.

HOURS LATER THE OLD MAN REACHES HOME...

GRANDFATHER! WHAT'S THE MATTER?

A ROMAN SOLDIER MADE HIM CARRY A HEAVY CHEST TO HEROD'S PALACE.

11

THAT AFTERNOON -- AS THE JEWS IN JERUSALEM GATHER IN THE TEMPLE FOR PRAYER -- AN OLD PRIEST, ZACHARIAS, ENTERS THE HOLY PLACE TO PRAY AND OFFER INCENSE.

THIS IS THE GREATEST DAY IN MY LIFE. AFTER ALL THESE YEARS IT IS FINALLY MY TURN TO OFFER INCENSE ON GOD'S HOLY ALTAR.

HE STAYS SO LONG IN THE SECRET ROOM THAT THE PEOPLE BEGIN TO WONDER.

ZACHARIAS' PRAYER IS LONGER THAN THAT OF MOST PRIESTS.

HE IS A GOOD MAN. IT'S TOO BAD HE HAS NO SON TO TAKE HIS PLACE.

AT LAST ZACHARIAS COMES OUT AND FACES THE PEOPLE -- BUT HE CANNOT SPEAK!

WHAT HAPPENED IN THE HOLY PLACE OF GOD?

A SON! AND HE WILL PREPARE THE WAY FOR GOD'S CHOSEN ONE!

BUT, ZACHARIAS, WHY DO YOU WRITE THIS INSTEAD OF TELLING ME?

ZACHARIAS WRITES A SECOND MESSAGE AND GIVES IT TO HIS WIFE.

GOD FORGIVE ME. I DOUBTED THE ANGEL'S MESSAGE, AND HE TOLD ME I WOULD NOT BE ABLE TO SPEAK UNTIL THE MESSAGE CAME TRUE.

OVERJOYED--AND AWED BY THE GREAT TRUST GOD HAS PLACED IN THEM-- ZACHARIAS AND ELISABETH PREPARE FOR THE BIRTH OF THEIR SON. IN THE MONTHS THAT PASS THEY OFTEN READ TOGETHER THE PARTS OF SCRIPTURE THAT TELL ABOUT GOD'S PROMISES TO HIS PEOPLE.

AS THE AGED PRIEST AND HIS WIFE WAIT FOR THE COMING OF THEIR SON, THE ANGEL GABRIEL APPEARS TO ELISABETH'S COUSIN MARY, WHO IS ENGAGED TO JOSEPH, A CARPENTER, IN NAZARETH.

DO NOT BE AFRAID, MARY. GOD HAS CHOSEN YOU TO BE THE MOTHER OF HIS SON. HIS NAME WILL BE "JESUS." HE WILL BE A KING WHOSE REIGN WILL NEVER END.

I AM THE LORD'S SERVANT AND I WILL DO WHATEVER HE SAYS.

14

MARY TELLS NO ONE OF THE ANGEL'S MESSAGE, BUT IN A FEW DAYS SHE GOES TO THE CARPENTER SHOP TO SEE JOSEPH.

I HAVE DECIDED TO GO AND VISIT MY COUSIN, ELISABETH.

IN JUDAH? I HATE TO HAVE YOU GO ALONE, MARY. IF ONLY THE PERIOD OF OUR ENGAGEMENT WERE OVER AND WE WERE MARRIED, THEN I COULD TAKE YOU THERE.

BUT, MARY LEAVES NAZARETH ALONE.

THE ANGEL SAID THAT ELISABETH IS GOING TO HAVE A SON, TOO. IT WILL BE GOOD TO TALK WITH HER.

AND WHEN SHE REACHES HER COUSIN...

MARY, HOW WONDERFULLY GOD HAS BLESSED YOU! BUT, TELL ME, WHY HAS THE MOTHER OF MY LORD COME TO VISIT ME?

FROM THIS GREETING MARY KNOWS THAT ELISABETH SHARES HER WONDERFUL SECRET. JOYFULLY SHE SINGS ALOUD HER PRAISE TO GOD.

MY SOUL DOTH MAGNIFY THE LORD... FOR HE THAT IS MIGHTY HATH DONE TO ME GREAT THINGS; AND HOLY IS HIS NAME.

15

OUR BIBLE IN PICTURES
A Father's Prophecy
FROM LUKE 1: 57-80; 2: 1-5

THE DAYS PASS SWIFTLY IN THE HOME OF THE OLD PRIEST, ZACHARIAS. HIS WIFE, ELISABETH AND HER YOUNG COUSIN, MARY, SPEND MANY HOURS TALKING ABOUT THE SONS GOD HAS PROMISED THEM. WHEN ELISABETH AND ZACHARIAS' CHILD IS BORN, NEIGHBORS AND RELATIVES COME TO SEE HIM.

HOW PROUD ZACHARIAS MUST BE TO HAVE A SON TO BEAR HIS NAME.

HE IS PROUD TO HAVE A SON, BUT, THE CHILD'S NAME IS JOHN.

JOHN? THEN YOU AREN'T NAMING HIM FOR ANYONE IN YOUR FAMILY?

ZACHARIAS -- WHO HAS NOT BEEN ABLE TO SPEAK A WORD SINCE HE DOUBTED THE ANGEL'S MESSAGE ABOUT THE BIRTH OF HIS SON -- MOTIONS FOR A TABLET. QUICKLY HE WRITES HIS ANSWER, AND HANDS IT TO THE WOMAN TO READ.

HIS NAME IS JOHN.

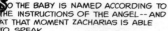

SO THE BABY IS NAMED ACCORDING TO THE INSTRUCTIONS OF THE ANGEL -- AND AT THAT MOMENT ZACHARIAS IS ABLE TO SPEAK.

BLESSED BE THE LORD GOD OF ISRAEL; FOR HE HATH VISITED AND REDEEMED HIS PEOPLE... AND THOU, CHILD, SHALT BE CALLED THE PROPHET OF THE HIGHEST: FOR THOU SHALT GO BEFORE THE FACE OF THE LORD TO PREPARE HIS WAYS.

ON THEIR WAY HOME THE PEOPLE TALK ABOUT THE STRANGE EVENTS CONNECTED WITH THE BIRTH OF ZACHARIAS' SON.

THE NAME JOHN -- WHAT DOES IT MEAN?

IT MEANS, "GOD HAS BEEN GRACIOUS." GOD MUST HAVE A SPECIAL PURPOSE FOR THAT CHILD.

HOME AGAIN IN NAZARETH, MARY THINKS ABOUT THE PURPOSE GOD HAS FOR HER CHILD. BUT JOSEPH, THE CARPENTER TO WHOM SHE IS ENGAGED, DOES NOT UNDERSTAND WHAT THE ANGEL HAS TOLD MARY ABOUT THE SON THAT IS TO BE BORN. ONE NIGHT AN ANGEL COMES TO HIM.

GOD HAS CHOSEN MARY TO BE THE MOTHER OF HIS SON. YOU MUST CALL THE CHILD JESUS, FOR HE WILL SAVE HIS PEOPLE FROM THEIR SINS.

17

EARLY THE NEXT MORNING, JOSEPH HURRIES TO SEE MARY.

O MARY, IN A DREAM LAST NIGHT AN ANGEL TOLD ME THAT YOU ARE TO BE THE MOTHER OF THE LORD. I SEE NOW THAT GOD HAS CHOSEN ME TO TAKE CARE OF YOU AND YOUR SON.

SO MARY AND JOSEPH ARE MARRIED, AND MOVE INTO JOSEPH'S HOUSE BESIDE THE CARPENTER SHOP. IN THE EVENINGS WHEN THE DAY'S WORK IS DONE, THEY REST ON THE ROOF TOP--WATCHING THE STARS AND TALKING ABOUT GOD'S PROMISE TO MARY.

BUT ONE DAY JOSEPH COMES HOME FROM THE MARKET PLACE WITH BAD NEWS: CAESAR AUGUSTUS HAS ORDERED EVERYONE TO REGISTER HIS NAME AND PROPERTY. SINCE JOSEPH AND MARY ARE DESCENDANTS OF KING DAVID, JOSEPH MUST GO TO BETHLEHEM, THE CITY OF DAVID.

BUT I CAN'T GO NOW-- AND LEAVE YOU...

YOU MUST GO, JOSEPH, AND I'LL GO WITH YOU. DON'T WORRY--GOD WILL BE WITH US.

EAGER TO HAVE THE REGISTRATION OVER, THEY SET OUT. SOON OTHERS JOIN THEM ON THE WAY. BUT THE JOURNEY TAKES SEVERAL DAYS, AND AFTER A WHILE JOSEPH AND MARY FALL BEHIND-- UNTIL THEY ARE AMONG THE LAST TO REACH BETHLEHEM.

WE HAVE TRAVELED A LONG WAY AND MY WIFE IS VERY TIRED. I NEED A ROOM.

I'M SORRY, BUT BETHLEHEM IS CROWDED THESE DAYS. THERE'S NO ROOM HERE.

OUR BIBLE IN PICTURES
The Night the Angels Sang
FROM LUKE 2: 8-20

AFTER A TIRESOME JOURNEY FROM NAZARETH, JOSEPH AND MARY REACH BETHLEHEM. BUT THE CITY IS SO CROWDED THAT THERE IS NO ROOM FOR THEM IN THE INN.

MY WIFE IS GOING TO HAVE A CHILD-- SOON. HAVE YOU NO PLACE SHE CAN GO TO REST?

NOT THIS NIGHT. BUT, WAIT- THERE IS AN EMPTY PLACE IN MY STABLE, IF--

TAKE IT, JOSEPH. IT IS LATE, AND I'M VERY TIRED.

MARY, THIS IS NO PLACE FOR YOU.

IT'S ALL RIGHT, JOSEPH. I'M THANKFUL FOR WHATEVER SHELTER WE CAN FIND.

THAT SAME NIGHT SOME SHEPHERDS ARE WATCHING THEIR SHEEP ON THE HILLS OUTSIDE THE CITY. THEY TALK OF THE CROWDS THAT HAVE COME TO BETHLEHEM.

I'VE HEARD THAT CAESAR AUGUSTUS ORDERED THIS REGISTRATION SO THAT HE CAN COLLECT MORE TAXES. WILL WE NEVER BE FREE FROM THESE FOREIGN TYRANTS?

GOD HAS PROMISED US A DELIVERER. AND ALL MY LIFE I HAVE PRAYED THAT I WOULD LIVE TO SEE HIM.

SUDDENLY-- A GREAT LIGHT SHINES AROUND THE SHEPHERDS.

WHAT IS IT?

O GOD, PROTECT US.

FEAR NOT; FOR I BRING YOU GOOD NEWS OF GREAT JOY FOR ALL THE PEOPLE. FOR TO YOU IS BORN IN THE CITY OF DAVID A SAVIOR, WHO IS CHRIST THE LORD. YOU WILL FIND THE BABY LYING IN A MANGER.

THEN THE SKY IS FILLED WITH A GREAT CHOIR OF ANGELS -- SINGING THEIR PRAISE TO GOD.

Glory to God in the highest, and on earth peace, good will toward men.

THE ANGELS LEAVE -- THE BEAUTIFUL LIGHT DISAPPEARS. ONCE AGAIN IT IS DARK AND STILL ON THE BETHLEHEM HILLS.

I CAN SCARCELY BELIEVE WHAT I HAVE SEEN AND HEARD. GOD HAS SENT OUR DELIVERER, OUR SAVIOR--**TONIGHT!**

AND TO THINK HE SENT HIS ANGEL TO TELL POOR SHEPHERDS LIKE US!

THE ANGEL SAID WE WOULD FIND THE SAVIOR IN A MANGER. LET'S GO TO BETHLEHEM AND SEE HIM.

EAGERLY -- AND WITH AWE AND WONDER -- THE SHEPHERDS HURRY TO BETHLEHEM. INSIDE THE GATE THEY TURN TOWARD THE INN...

LOOK -- THERE'S A LIGHT IN THE STABLE!

OUR SAVIOR IS HERE! AND I'M GOING TO SEE HIM!

"Fear not . . . For unto you is born this day
. . . a Saviour, which is Christ the Lord" (Luke 2: 10, 11).

A King Is Born

FROM LUKE 2: 7, 16-20; MATTHEW 2: 1-8

IT IS A STRANGE AND HOLY NIGHT. WHILE THE CROWDED CITY OF BETHLEHEM SLEEPS, THE SON OF GOD IS BORN. LOVINGLY, MARY WRAPS HER BABY IN SWADDLING CLOTHES AND LAYS HIM IN A MANGER... AND THERE THE SHEPHERDS FIND HIM.

AN ANGEL TOLD US THAT THE SAVIOR HAS BEEN BORN. MAY WE SEE HIM?

MARY NODS, AND JOSEPH TURNS THE LAMP A LITTLE SO THAT ITS LIGHT FALLS ON THE MANGER. REVERENTLY THE SHEPHERDS LOOK AT THE BABY JESUS.

O GOD, WE THANK THEE FOR SENDING OUR SAVIOR, AND FOR LETTING US SEE HIM.

WHEN THE WISE MEN INQUIRE AT THE PALACE, KING HEROD-- WHO HAS COMMITTED MORE THAN ONE MURDER TO PROTECT HIS THRONE-- IS FRIGHTENED. HE CALLS FOR THE CHIEF PRIESTS AND SCRIBES.

IS THERE ANYTHING IN THE SACRED BOOKS TELLING ABOUT A BABY WHO WILL BECOME KING OF THE JEWS?

YES, THE SCRIPTURES SAY HE WILL BE BORN IN BETHLEHEM.

SECRETLY HEROD SENDS FOR THE WISE MEN AND ASKS THEM WHEN THEY SAW THE STAR AND HOW LONG IT TOOK THEM TO COME TO JERUSALEM. THEN HE SPEAKS VERY SLYLY.

LOOK FOR THE CHILD IN BETHLEHEM. WHEN YOU FIND HIM, COME BACK AND TELL ME WHERE HE IS SO THAT I MAY WORSHIP HIM, TOO.

AND WHEN I FIND THAT CHILD, I'LL KILL HIM. NO ONE IS GOING TO BE KING OF THE JEWS BUT ME!

Flight in the Night

FROM MATTHEW 2: 9-14

FOLLOWING HEROD'S INSTRUCTIONS, THE WISE MEN SET OUT FOR BETHLEHEM. AS THEY LEAVE JERUSALEM, THEY AGAIN SEE THE STAR THEY HAD SEEN IN THE EAST. IT LEADS THEM TO BETHLEHEM, AND THERE...

LOOK! THE STAR HAS STOPPED ABOVE THAT HOUSE!

OUR JOURNEY IS FINISHED! SOON WE'LL SEE THE CHILD WHO IS TO BE KING OF THE JEWS!

PEOPLE IN BETHLEHEM ARE SURPRISED TO SEE THE IMPORTANT-LOOKING STRANGERS STOP BEFORE THE HOUSE WHERE JOSEPH AND MARY NOW LIVE. WHEN THE WISE MEN TELL THEIR REASON FOR COMING, THEY ARE INVITED INSIDE. THERE THEY KNEEL BEFORE THE BABY JESUS.

WE HAVE COME A LONG WAY TO WOR-SHIP THE ROYAL CHILD.

AND TO BRING HIM GIFTS OF GOLD, FRANKINCENSE, AND MYRRH.

THAT NIGHT AT THE INN THE WISE MEN MAKE PLANS FOR THEIR RETURN HOME.

I'M GLAD THAT WE CAN GO BACK TO JERUSALEM AND TELL KING HEROD WHERE HE CAN FIND THE BABY.

THE NEXT MORNING...

I HAD A DREAM—

SO DID I! IN MY DREAM GOD WARNED US NOT TO RETURN TO JERUSALEM BECAUSE HEROD IS JEALOUS AND WANTS TO KILL THE CHILD.

I HAD THE SAME DREAM! HEROD WILL FIND OUT NOTHING FROM US. WE'LL GO HOME BY ANOTHER ROUTE.

BUT THE WISE MEN ARE NOT THE ONLY ONES WHO ARE WARNED OF HEROD'S ANGER. AN ANGEL OF GOD APPEARS TO JOSEPH, TOO...

MARY! AN ANGEL HAS TOLD ME WE MUST ESCAPE AT ONCE -- TO EGYPT. HEROD WANTS TO KILL JESUS.

KILL JESUS! OH, NO!

IN THE MIDDLE OF THE NIGHT, JOSEPH AND MARY WITH THE BABY JESUS STEAL QUIETLY OUT OF THE CITY.

IN JERUSALEM, HEROD WAITS FOR THE RETURN OF THE WISE MEN. WHEN THEY DO NOT COME, HE SUSPECTS THEY ARE TRYING TO PROTECT THE CHILD -- FROM HIM.

THAT CHILD WILL NEVER LIVE TO TAKE MY THRONE. I'LL KILL EVERY BABY IN BETHLEHEM BEFORE I LET HIM ESCAPE.

28

AT HOME IN PALESTINE

THIS IS A TYPICAL HOME IN PALESTINE AT THE TIME OF JESUS. THE HOUSE IS MADE OF SUN-BAKED BRICKS. POORER PEOPLE LIVED IN HOUSES MADE OF CLAY. THE HEAVY, WOODEN DOOR ON THE STREET LEVEL WAS SELDOM OPENED. IN GOOD WEATHER THE FAMILY SPENT MUCH TIME ON THE ROOF WHICH WAS REACHED BY AN OUTSIDE STAIRWAY.

HOUSEHOLD TASKS, COOKING AND EATING, EVEN DRYING GRAIN, DATES AND GRAPES WERE DONE ON THE ROOF. JESUS SPOKE OF PREACHING FROM THE HOUSETOPS. (MATTHEW 10:27)

SINCE THE HOUSES WERE BUILT CLOSE TOGETHER, IT WAS AN EASY WAY OF TALKING TO ONE'S NEIGHBORS

MOST HOUSES OF WEALTHY PEOPLE WERE MADE OF BRICK OR PLASTERED MUD BAKED HARD. STONE WAS SELDOM USED BECAUSE THE MORTAR OFTEN BECAME LIKE SOAP AFTER A HEAVY RAIN. WHOLE PALESTINE VILLAGES HAVE BEEN WRECKED BY A SINGLE RAINSTORM.

WORKMEN MADE BRICKS BY MIXING MUD WITH STRAW. THIS WAS POURED INTO MOULDS AND BAKED HARD BY THE SUN OR IN LARGE OVENS KNOWN AS KILNS.

MARK 2:4 TELLS OF A SICK MAN BEING LOWERED THROUGH A ROOF SO THAT HE COULD SEE JESUS. THIS WAS POSSIBLE TO DO SINCE THE ROOFS WERE CONSTRUCTED SIMPLY OF RAFTERS WITH A LAYER OF TILE OVER THEM.

FOR COOLNESS, PALESTINE HOMES HAD ONLY A COUPLE OF WINDOWS—HEAVILY BARRED TO KEEP OUT ROBBERS. IF YOU FORGOT YOUR KEYS YOU COULD KNOCK A HOLE IN THE MUD WALL AND EASILY REPAIR IT WITH MORE MUD!

BEHIND CLOSED DOORS

MOST HOMES IN PALESTINE HAD TWO FLOORS. THE PEOPLE USED THEIR FLAT ROOFS FOR MANY ACTIVITIES, BUT THE SECOND FLOOR WAS THEIR MAIN LIVING QUARTERS. HERE THEY SLEPT AT NIGHT, DID THEIR COOKING, AND STORED THEIR BELONGINGS. IN THIS PICTURE WE SEE A TYPICAL FAMILY IN THE SECOND FLOOR OF THEIR HOME.

FATHER IS BRINGING HOME A SACK OF WHEAT. THE GIRL AND BOY ARE GRINDING FLOUR. MOTHER IS TAKING SOMETHING OUT OF ONE OF THE "CLOSETS" (THEIR CLOSETS WERE JUST "PIGEON HOLES" IN THE MUD WALLS). THE FIRE IS A LARGE HOLE IN THE FLOOR, FILLED WITH BURNING CHARCOAL.

WHEN IT'S TIME FOR BED AND THE FIRE HAS DIED DOWN TO A FEW GLOWING COALS, A BOARD WILL BE LAID OVER IT AND THEN A CARPET. THIS KEEPS THE ROOM WARM FOR HOURS. THE FAMILY SLEEPS ON MATTRESSES SPREAD ON THE FLOOR.

Homes in Palestine contained very little furniture. A few mats on the earthen or stone floor, a table or two, perhaps a couch, a bronze or pottery brazier (charcoal stove) was enough for their simple wants. When Mary and Martha entertained Jesus in their home *(Luke 10:38-42)* it probably looked like this.

The lower floor of the average house was used as a stable for animals when they couldn't be left outdoors. At other times it served as a workshop or a playroom.

There were no regular police, so doors and windows had to be heavily barred at night.

FAMILY FASHIONS
in the FIRST CENTURY

ONE THING TO BE SAID IN FAVOR OF THE CLOTHING STYLES IN JESUS' TIME IS THAT THEY DIDN'T CHANGE FROM YEAR TO YEAR AS OURS DO TODAY. PEOPLE NOW LIVING IN THAT PART OF THE WORLD DRESS JUST ABOUT THE SAME AS THEY DID, 2000 YEARS AGO...AND AS THEY HAD FOR HUNDREDS OF YEARS BEFORE JESUS WAS BORN.

ANOTHER POINT IN FAVOR OF THEIR CLOTHING WAS ITS SIMPLICITY...BOYS WORE A ONE-PIECE, SHORT-SLEEVED TUNIC WITH A V-NECK. IT WAS USUALLY HELD IN AT THE WAIST WITH A CORD OR A NARROW GIRDLE. THEY WORE THIS FOR WORK, PLAY, SCHOOL, AND AS A NIGHT SHIRT. NO EXCUSE FOR BEING LATE FOR BREAKFAST WITH THIS SIMPLE DRESSING PROBLEM!

GIRLS WORE THE SAME KIND OF CLOTHING AS THEIR MOTHERS WORE... WHICH, BY THE WAY, WAS PRACTICALLY THE SAME AS THE MEN WORE. IN FACT, SOME OF THE GARMENTS WERE SO MUCH ALIKE THAT THEY COULD BE WORN BY EITHER MEN OR WOMEN, AND NO ONE WOULD KNOW THE DIFFERENCE, EXCEPT FOR THE HEADDRESS. WOMEN AND GIRLS WORE LONG HEAD SCARFS.

LABORERS USUALLY WORE ONLY THE UNDERGARMENT—WITH OR WITHOUT SLEEVES—OR MERELY A WAIST-CLOTH WHICH REACHED TO THEIR KNEES.

FOR MORE FORMAL OCCASIONS THEY WORE A LONG-SLEEVED CLOAK OVER THEIR UNDERGARMENT.

A WIDE GIRDLE AROUND THEIR WAIST SERVED AS "POCKETS" IN WHICH THEY CARRIED MONEY, FOOD, A SWORD OR DAGGER, ETC.

SOME WORE A PLAIN SHEET WOUND AROUND THE BODY WITH ONE END FLUNG OVER THE SHOULDER. JESUS IS USUALLY PICTURED DRESSED THAT WAY.

PALESTINE STREETS WERE UNPAVED AND DUSTY. MOST PEOPLE HAD BASINS OF WATER HANDY IN THEIR HOMES IN WHICH GUESTS COULD WASH THEIR FEET. IT WAS A GREAT MARK OF HUMILITY AND RESPECT FOR THE HOST TO WASH HIS GUESTS' FEET. IN THE DESCRIPTION OF THE LAST SUPPER (JOHN 13:4-10) WE READ HOW JESUS WASHED THE FEET OF HIS DISCIPLES.

Boy in the Temple

FROM MATTHEW 2: 16-23; LUKE 2: 40-52

FEARING THAT THE BABY JESUS WILL TAKE HIS THRONE, HEROD ORDERS ALL BOY BABIES IN BETHLEHEM KILLED. BUT JOSEPH AND MARY ESCAPE WITH JESUS TO EGYPT. AFTER A FEW MONTHS, AN ANGEL TELLS JOSEPH THAT HEROD IS DEAD AND THAT IT IS NOW SAFE TO TAKE JESUS HOME. IN NAZARETH...

MARY! AND JOSEPH! HOW GOOD TO HAVE YOU BACK. WHAT IS THE BABY'S NAME?

HIS NAME IS JESUS.

JESUS. THE NAME MEANS "GOD SAVES." WE NEED SOMEONE TO SAVE US FROM THE TYRANTS WHO RULE PALESTINE.

JOSEPH SETS UP HIS CARPENTER SHOP--AND AS THE YEARS PASS, JESUS LEARNS TO HELP HIM. WHEN THE DAY'S WORK IS OVER JESUS LISTENS TO THE ELDERS OF THE TOWN...

IN THE DAYS OF KING DAVID, **WE** WERE THE RULERS.

YES, BUT IN THOSE DAYS PEOPLE OBEYED GOD. TODAY, TOO MANY IGNORE HIS LAWS.

BUT JOSEPH AND MARY OBEY GOD'S COMMANDMENTS, AND TEACH JESUS TO OBEY THEM, TOO. EACH SPRING THEY ATTEND THE PASSOVER FEAST IN JERU-SALEM TO THANK GOD FOR DELIVERING THEIR ANCESTORS FROM SLAVERY IN EGYPT. IN THE CARAVAN THAT MAKES THE ANNUAL JOURNEY FROM NAZARETH, THERE IS NO ONE MORE EXCITED THAN JESUS.

THIS YEAR, AS HE WORSHIPS IN THE TEMPLE, JESUS THINKS OF MANY QUESTIONS HE WOULD LIKE TO ASK THE TEACHERS OF THE JEWS.

AFTER THE FEAST IS OVER, THE PEOPLE SET OUT FOR THEIR HOMES. THAT NIGHT WHEN THEY MAKE CAMP...

JOSEPH, WHERE IS JESUS?

HE'S WITH HIS FRIENDS. I'LL FIND HIM.

BUT NO ONE HAS SEEN JESUS. FRANTICALLY, JOSEPH AND MARY TURN BACK TO JERUSALEM. THEY SEARCH THE INNS, THE CROWDED STREETS, AND FINALLY THE TEMPLE.

JESUS! WE HAVE BEEN LOOKING FOR YOU EVERYWHERE.

BUT, MOTHER, DIDN'T YOU KNOW THAT I WOULD BE IN MY FATHER'S HOUSE?

WE ARE SURPRISED AT YOUR SON'S KNOWLEDGE OF THE SCRIPTURES. HIS QUESTIONS SHOW THAT HE HAS THOUGHT A GREAT DEAL ABOUT GOD AND HIS LAWS FOR MAN.

JESUS IS NOT LIKE ANYONE ELSE. EVEN I, HIS MOTHER, DO NOT UNDERSTAND EVERYTHING ABOUT HIM.

JESUS RETURNS WITH JOSEPH AND MARY TO NAZARETH, WHERE HE LIVES UNTIL HE IS 30 YEARS OLD. HE GROWS TALL AND STRONG, AND IS WELL LIKED BY THE PEOPLE OF NAZARETH. GOD IS ALSO PLEASED WITH HIM. SEVENTY MILES AWAY, IN THE WILDERNESS NEAR THE DEAD SEA, A MAN OF THE SAME AGE PREPARES FOR AN ASSIGNMENT THAT WAS PLANNED FOR HIM -- EVEN BEFORE HE WAS BORN.

OUR BIBLE IN PICTURES

Tempted!

FROM LUKE 3: 1—4: 4

AS SOON AS JOHN, THE COUSIN OF JESUS, IS OLD ENOUGH TO UNDERSTAND, HIS FATHER TELLS HIM: "BEFORE YOU WERE BORN, GOD PLANNED FOR YOU TO SERVE HIM IN A SPECIAL WAY." JOHN GROWS UP PREPARING TO SERVE GOD. AND AFTER THE DEATH OF HIS PARENTS HE GOES INTO THE WILDERNESS TO PRAY AND STUDY. THERE GOD CALLS HIM TO BEGIN HIS WORK.

O GOD, I'M READY TO PREPARE THE WAY FOR THE COMING OF THE SAVIOR.

JOHN PUTS HIS WORDS INTO ACTION AND BEGINS PREACHING ALONG THE JORDAN RIVER.

REPENT OF YOUR SINS AND BE BAPTIZED, FOR GOD'S KINGDOM IS CLOSE AT HAND.

NEWS SPREADS FAR AND WIDE ABOUT THE MAN WHO LOOKS AND SPEAKS LIKE A PROPHET OF OLD. CROWDS COME OUT FROM JERUSALEM TO HEAR THE MAN CALLED JOHN THE BAPTIST. SOME ARE ONLY CURIOUS, BUT JOHN KNOWS THEIR THOUGHTS.

DO YOU THINK THAT JUST BECAUSE YOU ARE JEWS YOU WILL BE ALLOWED IN GOD'S KINGDOM? NO, YOU MUST REPENT--

THE SCOFFERS TURN AWAY, BUT MANY PEOPLE LISTEN EAGERLY. ONE DAY A CROWD GATHERS AT THE JORDAN RIVER.

ARE YOU THE SAVIOR GOD HAS PROMISED US?

NO. I BAPTIZE WITH WATER, BUT HE WILL BAPTIZE WITH THE HOLY SPIRIT OF GOD. PREPARE YOURSELVES; THE SAVIOR IS COMING!

UNKNOWN TO JOHN, THE VERY ONE HE IS TALKING ABOUT IS IN THE CROWD. JESUS HAS COME DOWN FROM NAZARETH TO HEAR HIM. HE ASKS TO BE BAPTIZED.

WHY DO YOU COME TO ME FOR BAPTISM? IT IS I WHO NEED TO BE BAPTIZED BY YOU.

IT IS GOOD, JOHN, FOR US TO SHOW THAT WE BELONG TO GOD'S KINGDOM.

39

So JOHN BAPTIZES JESUS. AND WHEN JESUS COMES UP OUT OF THE WATER, THE SPIRIT OF GOD DESCENDS LIKE A DOVE UPON HIM. THEN A VOICE FROM HEAVEN SPEAKS:

THIS IS MY BELOVED SON IN WHOM I AM WELL PLEASED.

THE CROWDS DO NOT UNDERSTAND WHAT HAS HAPPENED--THEY GO HOME, NOT REALIZING THAT THEY HAVE SEEN THEIR SAVIOR. JOHN CONTINUES PREACHING--REPENT OF YOUR SINS, FOR THE KINGDOM OF GOD IS COMING SOON.

To JESUS, THE WORDS OF HIS FATHER ARE A SIGN OF APPROVAL, AND THE GIFT OF THE HOLY SPIRIT IS AN ASSURANCE OF HELP FOR THE WORK GOD HAS SENT HIM TO DO. HE GOES INTO THE WILDERNESS-- ALONE--TO THINK ABOUT HIS PLAN FOR ESTABLISHING GOD'S KINGDOM.

At THE END OF FORTY DAYS, JESUS IS HUNGRY. AS HE THINKS OF FOOD, HE HEARS THE VOICE OF THE DEVIL TEMPTING HIM TO USE HIS DIVINE POWER FOR HIS OWN BENEFIT. "IF YOU ARE **REALLY** THE SON OF GOD," THE DEVIL SAYS, "TURN THIS STONE INTO BREAD. AFTER ALL, GOD WOULD NOT WANT HIS BELOVED SON TO BE HUNGRY."

SCRIPTURE SAYS, "MAN SHALL NOT LIVE BY BREAD ALONE, BUT BY THE WORD OF GOD."

THE DEVIL DOESN'T GIVE UP EASILY. HE TRIES AGAIN-- AND THIS TIME WITH A MORE POWERFUL TEMPTATION ...

Victory in the Wilderness

LUKE 4: 9-13; JOHN 1: 35-46

To prevent Jesus from carrying out God's work, the devil tempts him to seek earthly powers for himself. But Jesus refuses. The devil tries again -- this time he tempts Jesus to make himself popular by doing something sensational.

"Let people see your divine power by throwing yourself from the roof of the temple," the devil says. "For, if you are the son of God, his angels will take care of you."

The scriptures say, "Thou shalt not tempt God."

Having rejected every temptation, Jesus leaves the wilderness and goes back to Bethany beyond the Jordan.

AS JESUS ENTERS BETHANY, JOHN THE BAPTIST POINTS HIM OUT TO TWO OF HIS OWN DISCIPLES -- ANDREW AND JOHN.

THERE IS THE SAVIOR I HAVE BEEN TELLING YOU ABOUT.

THE TWO MEN TURN AND QUICKLY FOLLOW JESUS.

MASTER-- MAY WE TALK WITH YOU?

YES, COME WITH ME TO MY LODGING PLACE.

LISTENING TO JESUS IS SUCH A WONDERFUL EXPERIENCE THAT HOURS GO BY BEFORE ANDREW SUDDENLY REMEMBERS...

MY BROTHER! HE CAME DOWN HERE FROM CAPERNAUM WITH ME TO HEAR JOHN THE BAPTIST. I MUST FIND HIM AND BRING HIM TO SEE YOU.

ANDREW RUNS TO THE HOUSE WHERE HE AND HIS BROTHER ARE STAYING.

SIMON! I HAVE FOUND THE SAVIOR!

42

SIMON EAGERLY FOLLOWS ANDREW BACK THROUGH THE WINDING STREETS OF BETHANY.

THIS IS SIMON, MY BROTHER.

YES, YOU ARE SIMON, BUT FROM NOW ON YOU SHALL BE CALLED **PETER**, BECAUSE YOU WILL BE LIKE A ROCK.

THE NEXT DAY JESUS GOES NORTH TO GALILEE. HE INVITES ANOTHER YOUNG MAN, PHILIP, TO BE HIS DISCIPLE AND GO WITH HIM.

PHILIP ACCEPTS JESUS' INVITATION. LIKE ANDREW, HE WANTS TO SHARE HIS GOOD NEWS, SO HE HURRIES TO TELL A FRIEND.

NATHANAEL -- COME WITH ME! I HAVE FOUND THE SAVIOR! HE IS JESUS OF NAZARETH.

NAZARETH? CAN ANYTHING GOOD COME FROM **THAT** TOWN?

IF WHAT YOU SAY IS TRUE, MEN WOULD GIVE UP EVERYTHING THEY HAVE TO FOLLOW HIM.

COME AND SEE FOR YOURSELF!

NATHANAEL SEES JESUS, BUT HE STILL DOESN'T BELIEVE. THEN JESUS SPEAKS...

Six Jars of Water

FROM JOHN 1: 47-51; 2: 1-11, 23-25; 3: 1, 2

PHILIP IS SO EXCITED ABOUT SEEING JESUS THAT HE HURRIES TO TELL A FRIEND. "NATHANAEL, COME WITH ME. I HAVE FOUND THE SAVIOR!" NATHANAEL DOUBTS SUCH NEWS, BUT HE AGREES TO SEE FOR HIMSELF. AS THEY APPROACH JESUS...

BEHOLD, A MAN IN WHOM THERE IS NOTHING DECEITFUL.

HOW DO **YOU** KNOW ANYTHING ABOUT ME?

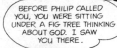

BEFORE PHILIP CALLED YOU, YOU WERE SITTING UNDER A FIG TREE THINKING ABOUT GOD. I SAW YOU THERE.

YOU **ARE** THE SAVIOR FOR WHOM WE HAVE WAITED SO LONG!

HAVING FOUND HIS SAVIOR, NATHANAEL FORGETS EVERYTHING ELSE AND JOINS JESUS AND HIS FRIENDS AS THEY TRAVEL NORTH TO GALILEE. AT THE CROSSROADS, PETER AND ANDREW TURN OFF TO THEIR HOME NEAR THE SEA OF GALILEE; THE OTHERS GO ON TO CANA.

WHEN THEY REACH THE TOWN, THEY ARE GREETED BY A FRIEND OF JESUS.

PLEASE COME TO MY WEDDING FEAST -- YOUR MOTHER WILL BE THERE.

THANK YOU -- WE WOULD LIKE TO SHARE YOUR HAPPINESS.

DURING THE FEAST MARY DISCOVERS SOMETHING THAT WILL EMBARRASS THE GROOM -- THERE IS NO MORE WINE. SHE TELLS JESUS, THEN SHE GOES TO THE SERVANTS.

DO WHATEVER HE TELLS YOU.

FILL THESE JARS WITH WATER.

WHY WATER? IT'S WINE WE NEED.

BUT THE SERVANTS SENSE A STRANGE AUTHORITY IN JESUS, AND THEY OBEY HIM.

NOW TAKE SOME TO THE HEADWAITER.

WHY -- IT IS WINE! IT'S A MIRACLE!

THIS MAN MUST BE A PROPHET OF GOD -- NO ORDINARY MAN COULD DO SUCH A THING!

45

THE HEADWAITER IS SO SURPRISED WHEN HE TASTES THE WINE THAT HE CALLS THE GROOM AWAY FROM THE FEAST.

SIR, THE BEST WINE IS USUALLY SERVED FIRST. BUT YOU HAVE SAVED THE BEST TO THE LAST.

I'M GLAD IF PEOPLE ARE HAPPY.

WHEN JESUS' DISCIPLES HEAR ABOUT THE MIRACLE, THEY TOO ARE EXCITED. THEY TALK ABOUT IT AS THEY GO DOWN TO JERUSALEM WITH JESUS FOR THE PASSOVER FEAST. THE CITY IS CROWDED WITH PEOPLE WHO HAVE HEARD JOHN THE BAPTIST TELL ABOUT THE COMING OF THE MESSIAH. "HOW WILL WE RECOGNIZE HIM?" THEY ASK.

AS JESUS WALKS THROUGH THE BUSY STREETS, HE HEALS THE LAME AND THE SICK.

I CAN WALK! PRAISE BE TO GOD -- THIS MAN HEALED ME!

BECAUSE OF THESE MIRACLES, PEOPLE BEGIN TO ASK: "IS JESUS THE MESSIAH?" ONE NIGHT, AFTER THE STREETS ARE EMPTY, A JUDGE OF THE JEWISH SUPREME COURT STEALS THROUGH THE STREETS OF JERUSALEM ON A SECRET MISSION.

THE CITY OF GATES

AT LEAST TWENTY GATES LEADING INTO JERUSALEM ARE RECORDED IN HISTORY. BECAUSE OF THE TRAFFIC PASSING THROUGH THEM, SOME OF THE GATES HAD COLORFUL NAMES SUCH AS FISH GATE, HORSE GATE, FOUNTAIN GATE, CORNER GATE, WATER GATE, SHEEP GATE AND SO ON. THE BUSY CARAVAN ROAD TO DAMASCUS ENTERED JERUSALEM THROUGH THE DAMASCUS GATE, PICTURED HERE.

THE WALLED CITY OF JERUSALEM ENDURED MORE THAN 20 SIEGES AND BLOCKADES. EIGHTEEN TIMES THE CITY AND ITS WALLS WERE COMPLETELY DESTROYED...AND REBUILT AGAIN. EVERY TIME NEW WALLS WERE SET UP, NEW GATES WERE CONSTRUCTED AND GIVEN NEW NAMES!

STAGGERED GATES WERE OFTEN SET IN DOUBLE WALLS AROUND A CITY, WITH A CORRIDOR ABOUT 30 FT. WIDE IN BETWEEN. AN ENEMY WHO GOT THROUGH THE OUTER GATE WAS FORCED TO TURN LEFT. AT THIS MOMENT, THE ENEMY HAD TO EXPOSE HIS RIGHT SIDE (UNPROTECTED BY A SHIELD) TO DEFENDERS ON THE WALLS.

The Judge's Problem

FROM JOHN 3: 3—4: 6

NICODEMUS, A JUDGE OF THE JEWISH SUPREME COURT, HAS A PROBLEM HE CAN'T SOLVE. PEOPLE IN JERUSALEM ARE ASKING, "IS JESUS THE SAVIOR WHO WILL OVERTHROW THE ROMANS AND SET UP GOD'S KINGDOM IN PALESTINE?" NICODEMUS ISN'T SURE, AND HE WONDERS: "WHAT MUST A MAN DO TO ENTER GOD'S KINGDOM?" HE HAS TO FIND OUT. SO SECRETLY-- BY NIGHT-- HE GOES TO THE PLACE WHERE JESUS IS STAYING, AND JESUS ANSWERS HIS QUESTION EVEN BEFORE HE ASKS IT...

A MAN MUST BE BORN OVER AGAIN TO ENTER GOD'S KINGDOM.

BORN AGAIN? HOW CAN I BE BORN AGAIN WHEN I AM OLD?

YOU WERE BORN ONCE OF EARTHLY PARENTS. BUT YOU MUST BE BORN AGAIN OF GOD'S SPIRIT TO LIVE IN GOD'S KINGDOM.

I DON'T UNDERSTAND.

YOU CAN'T SEE THE WIND, BUT YOU CAN SEE WHAT IT DOES. YOU CANNOT SEE THE SPIRIT OF GOD, BUT YOU CAN TELL BY THE WAY A MAN LIVES IF HE HAS BEEN BORN AGAIN AND HAS THE SPIRIT OF GOD IN HIS HEART. GOD LOVES THE WORLD, AND HE HAS SENT ME TO GIVE THIS NEW LIFE TO ALL WHO BELIEVE IN ME.

NICODEMUS GOES AWAY--STILL PUZZLED, BUT WANTING TO LEARN MORE ABOUT JESUS AND HIS TEACHINGS.

JESUS SEES THAT MANY OF THE PEOPLE IN JERUSALEM ARE NOT READY TO RECEIVE HIM AS THEIR SAVIOR, SO HE LEAVES THE CITY. IN JUDEA HE TELLS THE PEOPLE ABOUT GOD'S KINGDOM AND WHAT THEY MUST DO TO ENTER IT. HERE, THE PEOPLE LISTEN EAGERLY.

THIS TEACHER IS GREATER THAN ALL THE PROPHETS.

NEWS OF JESUS' SUCCESSFUL MINISTRY IN JUDEA REACHES JOHN THE BAPTIST.

I'VE HEARD THAT JESUS IS BECOMING MORE POPULAR EVERY DAY.

THANK GOD, I HAVE FULFILLED MY MISSION OF PREPARING THE WAY FOR HIM. JESUS' INFLUENCE MUST INCREASE, AND MINE DECREASE.

50

SOMETIME LATER JESUS RECEIVES NEWS ABOUT HIS LOYAL FRIEND.

HEROD HAS PUT JOHN THE BAPTIST IN PRISON FOR TRYING TO START A REVOLUTION.

REVOLUTION? NO-- THE REAL REASON IS THAT JOHN CONDEMNED HEROD FOR MARRYING HIS BROTHER'S WIFE.

SOON AFTER THIS, JESUS DECIDES TO EXTEND HIS MINISTRY INTO ANOTHER AREA. HE SETS OUT FOR GALILEE, NORTH OF SAMARIA

AS THEY APPROACH A TOWN IN SAMARIA, JESUS SENDS HIS DISCIPLES ON AHEAD TO BUY SOME FOOD.

IT MAY BE QUICKER TO GO TO GALILEE BY WAY OF SAMARIA, BUT I WONDER IF IT'S WISE. SAMARITANS HATE US JEWS.

WHILE JESUS IS RESTING BESIDE THE WELL, A WOMAN COMES UP WITH A JAR FOR WATER.

A JEW! DOESN'T HE KNOW JEWS AREN'T WELCOME IN SAMARIA?

51

WATER IN THE DESERT

PALESTINE VILLAGES HAD NO RUNNING WATER IN BIBLE TIMES. WELLS WERE THE ONLY SOURCE OF WATER, SO THEY WERE THE CENTERS OF VILLAGE ACTIVITY. WOMEN AND CHILDREN WENT EVERY DAY TO THE WELLS, CARRYING BIG WATER JARS ON THEIR HEADS. THIS IS A SCENE AT THE WELL IN NAZARETH, WHERE JESUS, AS A BOY, MUST HAVE GONE MANY TIMES WITH HIS MOTHER. MARY'S WELL IS STILL USED BY THE PEOPLE OF NAZARETH TODAY.

WATER AND WELLS ARE MENTIONED OFTEN IN THE BIBLE. JOHN 4:6 TELLS HOW JESUS TALKED TO THE WOMAN OF SAMARIA AT JACOB'S WELL NEAR SYCHAR.

In the palestine desert, ownership of wells meant the difference between life and death, so many battles were fought for possession of wells. Isaac did not want to fight other herdsmen about water, so he moved away and dug new wells (Genesis 26:12-35).

Water was brought into Jerusalem from outside wells through tunnels which ran underneath the city's thick walls. David once conquered the city by sending soldiers through these tunnels while the defenders stood on the walls.

Many a well was the scene of romance. Rachel first met Jacob when he "rolled the stone from the well's mouth" and helped her to water Laban's flocks (Genesis 29:10).

In Enemy Territory

FROM JOHN 4: 6-44; LUKE 4: 16-28

THE JEWS AND SAMARITANS HAVE BEEN BITTER ENEMIES FOR OVER 500 YEARS, SO WHEN JESUS ASKS A SAMARITAN WOMAN FOR A DRINK OF WATER SHE IS SURPRISED.

WHAT? YOU, A JEW, ASK ME, A SAMARITAN, FOR A DRINK?

IF YOU KNEW WHO I AM YOU WOULD ASK ME TO GIVE YOU LIVING WATER.

BUT THE WELL IS DEEP AND YOU HAVE NO WAY TO GET WATER.

ANYONE WHO DRINKS FROM THIS WELL WILL THIRST AGAIN, BUT THE PERSON WHO DRINKS OF THE WATER I GIVE WILL NEVER THIRST, FOR IT IS GOD'S GIFT OF ETERNAL LIFE.

WHEN JESUS TELLS HER THAT HE IS THE SAVIOR FROM GOD, SHE BELIEVES HIM AND RUNS BACK TO THE TOWN TO TELL THE WONDERFUL NEWS.

COME! SEE A MAN WHO HAS TOLD ME THINGS ABOUT MY LIFE THAT NO STRANGER COULD KNOW. HE IS THE PROMISED MESSIAH! THE SAVIOR!

WHILE THE WOMAN IS IN THE TOWN, JESUS' DISCIPLES RETURN AND INVITE HIM TO SHARE THE FOOD THEY HAVE BOUGHT.

THANK YOU, BUT NOT NOW-- I HAVE FOOD THAT YOU DON'T KNOW ABOUT.

WHAT DO YOU MEAN?

MY FOOD IS TO DO THE WILL OF HIM WHO SENT ME. LOOK AT THE PEOPLE WHO ARE EAGER TO HEAR WHAT GOD HAS SENT ME TO TELL THEM.

ALTHOUGH THE SAMARITANS HATE JEWS, MANY OF THEM BELIEVE JESUS TO BE THEIR SAVIOR. "STAY," THEY PLEAD, "AND TELL US MORE ABOUT GOD AND HIS KINGDOM." JESUS REMAINS FOR TWO DAYS-- THEN GOES ON TO THE REGION OF GALILEE.

ON THE SABBATH, IN HIS TOWN OF NAZARETH, HE GOES TO THE SYNAGOGUE. THERE HE READS FROM THE BOOK OF ISAIAH WHICH TELLS ABOUT THE COMING OF THE MESSIAH. THEN HE SITS DOWN TO TEACH.

TODAY THIS SCRIPTURE HAS BEEN FULFILLED IN YOUR EARS.

YOU -- THE MESSIAH? WHY, YOU'RE JUST THE SON OF A NAZARETH CARPENTER!

NO PROPHET IS ACCEPTED IN HIS OWN COUNTRY. REMEMBER -- IN THE DAYS OF ELISHA THERE WERE MANY LEPERS IN ISRAEL, BUT THE PROPHET HEALED ONLY ONE -- A FOREIGNER, NAAMAN.

THE THOUGHT THAT GOD WOULD DO MORE FOR FOREIGNERS THAN FOR THEM -- HIS CHOSEN PEOPLE -- TURNS THE WORSHIPERS INTO AN ANGRY MOB.

DRIVE HIM OUT OF THE CITY!

KILL HIM!

On a Nazareth Hill

FROM LUKE 4: 29-37; MARK 1: 16-31; 2: 1-3

THE MOB PUSHES JESUS OUT OF THE SYNAGOGUE... THROUGH THE STREETS... TO THE TOP OF A HILL. IN ALL THAT TIME JESUS MAKES NO MOVE TO STOP THE ANGRY CROWD.

THROW HIM DOWN!

BUT--SUDDENLY--JESUS TURNS AND LOOKS INTO THE FACES OF THE MEN AND WOMEN WHO HAVE KNOWN HIM FOR THIRTY YEARS. THEN HE WALKS--SLOWLY--THROUGH THEIR MIDST... AND, STRANGELY, NOT A PERSON DARES TO TOUCH HIM.

FROM NAZARETH JESUS GOES TO CAPERNAUM ON THE SEA OF GALILEE. THERE HE FINDS THE BROTHERS HE MET NEAR THE JORDAN RIVER.

PETER! ANDREW! COME WITH ME, AND I'LL MAKE YOU FISHERS OF MEN.

THEY LEAVE THEIR NETS AND GO AT ONCE WITH JESUS. FARTHER DOWN THE SHORE JESUS SEES TWO MORE FRIENDS--JAMES AND JOHN.

COME WITH ME AND BE MY DISCIPLES.

FATHER, WE MUST GO WITH JESUS AND HELP HIM IN THE WORK HE IS DOING FOR GOD.

GO, MY SONS, AND MAY GOD BLESS YOU.

WITH HIS DISCIPLES JESUS MAKES HIS HEADQUARTERS IN CAPERNAUM. ON THE SABBATH HE GOES TO THE SYNAGOGUE--AND WHILE HE IS TEACHING, A MAN POSSESSED BY AN EVIL SPIRIT CRIES OUT...

I KNOW WHO YOU ARE--THE HOLY ONE OF GOD. HAVE YOU COME TO DESTROY ME?

JESUS FEELS SORRY FOR THE MAN AND ORDERS THE EVIL SPIRIT TO COME OUT OF HIM.

LATER THAT DAY JESUS HEALS PETER'S MOTHER-IN-LAW, WHO HAS BEEN ILL WITH A FEVER. NEWS OF THESE MIRACLES SPREADS THROUGH THE COUNTRY, AND WHEREVER JESUS GOES GREAT CROWDS FOLLOW HIM. ONE DAY IN CAPERNAUM...

IT'S NO USE. YOU CAN NEVER GET ME THROUGH THAT MOB TO JESUS.

WHO IS THIS MAN WHO HAS POWER OVER EVIL SPIRITS?

I DON'T KNOW--BUT I'VE HEARD HE CAN CHANGE WATER INTO WINE AND MAKE THE LAME WALK

AND IF HE DOESN'T SEE JESUS, HE'LL NEVER BE WELL AGAIN.

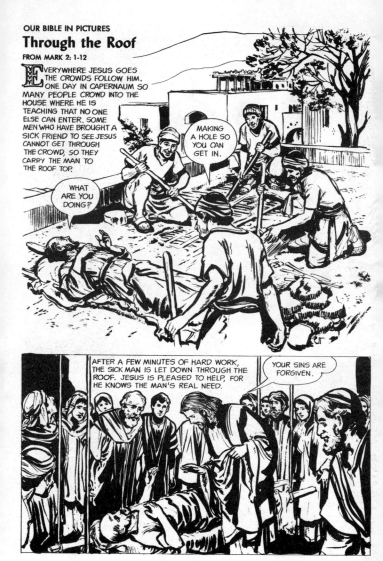

OUR BIBLE IN PICTURES

Through the Roof

FROM MARK 2: 1-12

EVERYWHERE JESUS GOES THE CROWDS FOLLOW HIM. ONE DAY IN CAPERNAUM SO MANY PEOPLE CROWD INTO THE HOUSE WHERE HE IS TEACHING THAT NO ONE ELSE CAN ENTER. SOME MEN WHO HAVE BROUGHT A SICK FRIEND TO SEE JESUS CANNOT GET THROUGH THE CROWD, SO THEY CARRY THE MAN TO THE ROOF TOP.

MAKING A HOLE SO YOU CAN GET IN.

WHAT ARE YOU DOING?

AFTER A FEW MINUTES OF HARD WORK, THE SICK MAN IS LET DOWN THROUGH THE ROOF. JESUS IS PLEASED TO HELP, FOR HE KNOWS THE MAN'S REAL NEED.

YOUR SINS ARE FORGIVEN.

THE PEOPLE ARE AMAZED. BUT THE PHARISEES,* WHO HAVE COME OUT OF CURIOSITY TO HEAR JESUS, ARE ANGRY.

WHO IS THIS MAN WHO PRETENDS TO FORGIVE SINS?

HOW DARE HE ACT AS IF HE IS GOD!

*The Pharisees are a group of Jews who believe in obeying not only the laws God gave to Moses but the hundreds of rules they have made--such as how far a man can walk on the Sabbath. Because Jesus is more concerned about helping people than obeying their rules, the Pharisees turn against him.

JESUS KNOWS WHAT THE PHARISEES ARE THINKING.

WHICH IS EASIER-- TO SAY TO THE SICK, "YOUR SINS ARE FORGIVEN," OR TO SAY, "ARISE, TAKE UP YOUR BED, AND WALK"?

BUT SO THAT ALL MAY KNOW THAT I HAVE DIVINE POWER TO DO BOTH, I SAY TO YOU, "ARISE, TAKE UP YOUR BED, AND GO TO YOUR HOME."

61

MY SINS ARE FORGIVEN! I'M HEALED! GLORY BE TO GOD!

I'VE NEVER SEEN ANYTHING LIKE IT.

NEITHER HAVE I. BUT IF HE IS TRYING TO MAKE US THINK HE IS THE MESSIAH, WHY DOESN'T HE DO SOMETHING ABOUT OVERTHROWING THE ROMANS?

JESUS LEAVES THE HOUSE WHERE HE HAS BEEN TEACHING, AND AS HE PASSES BY THE TOLL HOUSE AT THE CITY GATE...

YOU TAX COLLECTORS ARE ALL ROBBERS. I CAN'T PAY THAT MUCH TAX, AND YOU KNOW IT.

YOU'D BETTER PAY IT! REMEMBER — I HAVE THE POWER OF THE WHOLE ROMAN EMPIRE BEHIND ME.

Street Corner Secretary

Few people in Bible days knew how to write, so there was a need for public scribes. Here we see a merchant dictating a letter to a scribe who has set up his "office" right in the open near the city gate.

When the letter was finished it was sent to its destination by runners or given to travelers who were going that way. The sender put his mark on the letter and sealed it with a bit of wax.

Training for a scribe began when the boy was 13. He learned his trade at the school of a rabbi. The teacher and older pupils sat on raised platforms while the younger boys sat on mats on the floor.

This training took a long time. Not until he was about 30 years old was the scribe admitted to office. He could then be a public scribe... a doctor of the law... a teacher... a member of the Sanhedrin, the Jewish high court, or a transcriber, copying the law and the prophets for use in the synagogue.

Jesus read from such a copy of the book of Isaiah before the synagogue in Nazareth, LUKE 4:16-20.

No Traffic Lights!

STREETS OF BIBLE-TIME TOWNS WERE USUALLY NARROW, CROWDED AND NOISY. THEY WOUND THEIR WAY THROUGH THE CITY, TWISTING AND TURNING UPHILL AND DOWN. THROUGH THESE STREETS WENT MERCHANTS WITH THEIR HEAVILY LOADED CAMELS, HORSES AND DONKEYS...PORTERS CARRYING HEAVY BUNDLES ON THEIR BACKS ...WOMEN BALANCING WATER JARS ON THEIR HEADS...BEGGARS...PEDDLERS— ALL PUSHING, BUMPING AND JOSTLING.

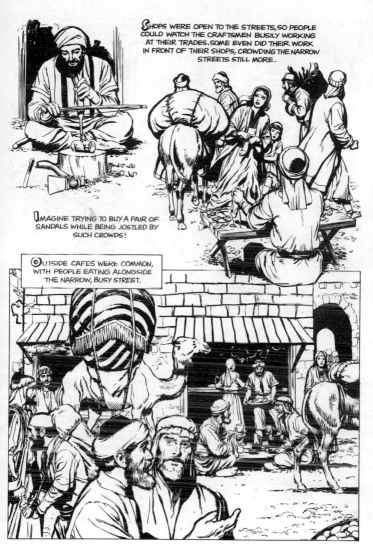

SHOPS WERE OPEN TO THE STREETS, SO PEOPLE COULD WATCH THE CRAFTSMEN BUSILY WORKING AT THEIR TRADES. SOME EVEN DID THEIR WORK IN FRONT OF THEIR SHOPS, CROWDING THE NARROW STREETS STILL MORE.

IMAGINE TRYING TO BUY A PAIR OF SANDALS WHILE BEING JOSTLED BY SUCH CROWDS!

OUTSIDE CAFES WERE COMMON, WITH PEOPLE EATING ALONGSIDE THE NARROW, BUSY STREET.

When an important person traveled through the streets in a chariot, a runner always came first to clear a way.

And the streets teemed with beggars, cripples and blind people. Jesus referred to these poor unfortunates in his parable of the marriage supper in Luke 14:21.

The busy streets were a bedlam of noise... peddlers shouting their wares, merchants haggling over prices, tradesmen advertising their goods. Not until darkness fell did the streets quiet down.

SPREAD-OUT SUPERMARKETS

When you go to a supermarket today you go to the right section and choose the food you want. But in Bible days all the shops that sold bread would be on "bakers' street,"... all the meat shops on "butchers' row,"... candy shops on "the street of sweets."

So shopping in those days meant a lot of walking from street to street.

THERE WERE NO CHECK-OUT COUNTERS, EITHER. MERCHANTS FIGURED THE TOTAL AMOUNT DUE ON AN ABACUS...AN ANCIENT "ADDING MACHINE" STILL USED IN THE ORIENT TODAY.

THERE WERE NO PRICE TAGS. WHAT YOU PAID WAS DETERMINED BY HOW GOOD YOU WERE AT BARGAINING AND HOW ANXIOUS THE MERCHANT WAS TO MAKE A SALE.

PALESTINE DAYS WERE HOT. AFTER A MERCHANT HAD OPENED HIS SHOP AND SPREAD OUT HIS WARES, HE WOULD GO INTO THE BACK AND SNOOZE UNTIL A PROSPECTIVE CUSTOMER AROUSED HIM—OR ONE OF HIS RICKETY STANDS WAS KNOCKED OVER BY A PASSING SHOPPER OR CAMEL IN THE NARROW CROWDED STREETS.

SOMETIMES FOREIGN TRADERS WOULD HAVE A SPECIAL QUARTER OF THE CITY SET APART FOR THEM. USUALLY, HOWEVER, TRAVELING TRADESMEN DISPLAYED THEIR WARES BOTH IN AND OUTSIDE OF THE CITY'S GATES.

A SHEKEL COINED ABOUT 140 B.C.

THE SHEKEL WAS THE MOST COMMON COIN USED IN PALESTINE IN BIBLE DAYS. A GOLD SHEKEL WAS WORTH ABOUT $10 IN OUR MONEY. A SILVER SHEKEL ABOUT 60-75 CENTS. ONE HALF AND ONE QUARTER SILVER SHEKELS WERE ALSO USED.

MANY SHOPS IN PALESTINE WERE UNTIDY AND UNSANITARY, BUT JEWISH LAW WAS STRICT ABOUT SOME THINGS. A WHOLESALE DEALER HAD TO CLEAN HIS SCALE OR MEASURES ONCE A MONTH—A RETAIL DEALER, TWICE A WEEK. ALL WEIGHTS HAD TO BE WASHED ONCE A MONTH AND THE BALANCES WIPED CLEAN EVERY TIME THEY WERE USED.

WELCOME TO CHORAZIN THE GRAIN CITY

JESUS REFERRED TO HIS DISCIPLES HAVING GONE TO THE CITY TO BUY FOOD WHEN HE SPOKE TO THE WOMAN AT THE WELL OF SAMARIA. (JOHN 4:8)

MANY CITIES WERE GIVEN OVER ENTIRELY TO MAKING JUST ONE PRODUCT. FOR EXAMPLE, MAGDALA WAS KNOWN AS "THE CITY OF DYERS." BETHSAIDA (THE HOME OF JESUS' DISCIPLES, PHILIP, ANDREW AND PETER) WAS FAMOUS FOR ITS FISHING INDUSTRY.

OUR BIBLE IN PICTURES
One Man's Answer
FROM MATTHEW 9: 9-13; 12: 9-14

IN ALL CAPERNAUM THERE IS NO JEW MORE DESPISED THAN MATTHEW, A TAX COLLECTOR FOR ROME. ONE DAY AS HE AND A MERCHANT ARE ARGUING ABOUT TAXES ON A CARAVAN OF GOODS, JESUS PASSES BY. HE LOOKS STRAIGHT INTO THE EYES OF THE HATED TAX COLLECTOR...

MATTHEW, FOLLOW ME.

TO THE AMAZEMENT OF THE CROWD, MATTHEW TURNS FROM HIS WORK AND FOLLOWS JESUS.

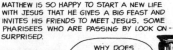

I CAN'T BELIEVE IT! MATTHEW IS GIVING UP HIS JOB TO GO WITH A MAN OF GOD!

STRANGE-- NO GOOD JEW EVER WANTED MATTHEW FOR A FRIEND.

MATTHEW IS SO HAPPY TO START A NEW LIFE WITH JESUS THAT HE GIVES A BIG FEAST AND INVITES HIS FRIENDS TO MEET JESUS. SOME PHARISEES WHO ARE PASSING BY LOOK ON-- SURPRISED.

WHY DOES YOUR MASTER EAT WITH ALL THOSE SINNERS?

JESUS ANSWERS FOR HIS DISCIPLE.

ONLY THE SICK NEED A DOCTOR. I HAVE COME NOT TO CALL THE RIGHTEOUS BUT SINNERS TO REPENT.

THE PHARISEES HAVE NO ANSWER TO THIS--BUT IT MAKES THEM EVEN MORE ANGRY. SO EVERYWHERE JESUS GOES THEY WATCH FOR A CHANCE TO CRITICIZE HIM. ONE SABBATH DAY IN THE SYNAGOGUE...

LOOK--JESUS IS TALKING TO THAT MAN WITH THE WITHERED HAND. LET'S SEE IF WE CAN CATCH HIM BREAKING A SABBATH LAW. THEN WE'LL HAVE A CASE AGAINST HIM.

72

ermon on the Mount

OM LUKE 6: 12-16; MATTHEW 5; 6; 7; 8: 5-13; 13: 45, 46;
ARK 4: 35-37

JESUS KNOWS THAT THE PHARISEES ARE PLOTTING TO TAKE HIS LIFE, BUT HE DOES NOT LET THIS KEEP HIM FROM CARRYING ON THE WORK GOD SENT HIM TO DO. HE GOES TO A NEARBY MOUNTAIN-- AND SPENDS THE NIGHT IN PRAYER...

...AND FATHER, I THANK THEE FOR GUIDING ME IN THE CHOICES I HAVE MADE THIS NIGHT.

IN THE MORNING HE CALLS HIS DISCIPLES TO HIM--AND FROM THE GROUP HE NAMES TWELVE TO BE HIS FULL TIME HELPERS: SIMON PETER, ANDREW, JAMES, JOHN, PHILIP, NATHANAEL BARTHOLOMEW, MATTHEW, THOMAS, JAMES THE SON OF ALPHEUS, THADDEUS, SIMON THE ZEALOT, AND JUDAS ISCARIOT. THESE ARE KNOWN AS THE TWELVE APOSTLES.

73

As they come down the mountain they find a large crowd waiting for Jesus. So there--on the mountainside--Jesus preaches a sermon in which he explains what members of God's kingdom are like:

Blessed are the merciful: for they shall obtain mercy.

Blessed are the pure in heart: for they shall see God.

Blessed are the peacemakers: for they shall be called the children of God....

Ye are the light of the world.... Let your light so shine before men, that they may see your good works, and glorify your Father which is in heaven....

Love your enemies, bless them that curse you, do good to them that hate you, and pray for them which despitefully use you, and persecute you;

That ye may be the children of your Father which is in heaven: for he maketh his sun to rise on the evil and on the good, and sendeth rain on the just and on the unjust....

Therefore all things whatsoever ye would that men should do to you, do ye even so to them: for this is the law and the prophets.

(The full sermon is found in Matthew, chapters 5, 6, 7.)

74

AFTER THE SERMON JESUS TAKES HIS DISCIPLES BACK TO CAPERNAUM, AS THEY ENTER THE CITY THEY ARE STOPPED BY AN OFFICER OF THE ROMAN ARMY.

JESUS! MY SERVANT IS ILL. WILL YOU PLEASE MAKE HIM WELL?

I WILL GO WITH YOU.

I'M NOT WORTHY TO HAVE YOU COME TO MY HOUSE -- BUT I KNOW THAT IF YOU SAY THE WORD MY SERVANT WILL BE HEALED.

NOWHERE IN ALL ISRAEL HAVE I SEEN A MAN WITH SUCH FAITH. GO BACK TO YOUR SERVANT-- AND AS YOU BELIEVE, SO IT WILL BE.

THE OFFICER HURRIES HOME.

MASTER! LOOK! I'M WELL. IT HAPPENED-- SUDDENLY-- JUST A FEW MINUTES AGO.

AREN'T YOU SURPRISED?

NO -- BECAUSE I BELIEVED THAT JESUS WOULD HEAL YOU.

EVEN THOUGH THE PHARISEES ARE STILL PLOTTING AGAINST HIM, JESUS KEEPS ON TEACHING IN CAPERNAUM. ONE DAY THE CROWDS THAT COME TO HEAR HIM ARE SO GREAT THAT HE HAS TO GET INTO A BOAT AND PUSH OUT FROM SHORE IN ORDER TO TEACH THEM.

A MERCHANT ONCE SAW A RARE AND BEAUTIFUL PEARL. HE WANTED IT MORE THAN ANYTHING ELSE. SO HE SOLD EVERYTHING HE OWNED AND BOUGHT IT. THE KINGDOM OF GOD IS LIKE THAT PEARL-- IT IS WORTH EVERYTHING YOU HAVE TO POSSESS IT.

WHEN EVENING COMES JESUS SUGGESTS TO HIS DISCIPLES THAT THEY CROSS OVER TO THE OTHER SIDE OF THE LAKE.

IT'S THE KIND OF A NIGHT WHEN A SUDDEN STORM COULD HIT.

IN TERROR THE DISCIPLES RUSH TO THE STERN OF THE BOAT.

MASTER! DON'T YOU CARE IF WE DROWN?

JESUS RISES AND FACES THE STORMY SEA

PEACE, BE STILL!

INSTANTLY THE WIND DIES AND THE WAVES VANISH.

WHO IS HE, THAT EVEN THE WINDS AND THE SEA OBEY HIM?

IN THE MORNING THE BOAT REACHES SHORE; AND AS JESUS AND HIS DISCIPLES ARE WALKING UP THE BEACH, A MAN POSSESSED BY AN EVIL SPIRIT RUSHES DOWN THE BANK TO MEET JESUS.

BE CAREFUL! HE'S BROKEN HIS CHAINS.

COME OUT OF THE MAN, THOU UNCLEAN SPIRIT.

THE MAN IS CURED -- THE PEOPLE WHO SEE IT ARE AMAZED, AND THEY WONDER, TOO, WHAT POWER JESUS HAS TO MAKE EVIL SPIRITS OBEY HIM.

LET ME GO WITH YOU.

IT WOULD BE BETTER IF YOU WENT HOME AND TOLD YOUR FRIENDS WHAT GOD HAS DONE FOR YOU.

AFTER A WHILE JESUS AND HIS DISCIPLES RETURN TO CAPERNAUM. ONCE AGAIN A CROWD GATHERS TO HEAR HIM. BUT JUST AS JESUS BEGINS TO TEACH, JAIRUS, THE CHIEF RULER OF THE SYNAGOGUE, PUSHES HIS WAY THROUGH THE CROWD AND FALLS AT JESUS' FEET.

MY LITTLE GIRL -- SHE'S DYING! PLEASE COME!

JESUS GOES WITH JAIRUS -- BUT ON THE WAY THEY ARE MET BY A SERVANT FROM JAIRUS' HOUSEHOLD...

IT'S TOO LATE YOUR DAUGHTER IS DEAD!

The Mocking Crowd

FROM MARK 5: 38-43; MATTHEW 9: 35—11: 1; 14: 1-12; JOHN 6: 1-10

WHEN JESUS AND HIS DISCIPLES REACH THE HOME OF JAIRUS, THEY FIND A CROWD OF PEOPLE WEEPING BECAUSE JAIRUS' DAUGHTER IS DEAD.

WHY ARE YOU CRYING? THE LITTLE GIRL IS JUST ASLEEP.

ASLEEP? HOW DARE YOU RAISE FALSE HOPE FOR THIS FAMILY? THE CHILD IS DEAD, AND EVERYONE KNOWS IT!

QUIETLY JESUS LEADS THE CHILD'S PARENTS INTO HER ROOM. THERE HE TAKES THE GIRL'S HAND AND SAYS, "ARISE." INSTANTLY SHE GETS UP-- AND LOOKS AT JESUS IN SURPRISE AND WONDER.

GIVE HER SOMETHING TO EAT-- BUT DO NOT TELL ANYONE WHAT HAS HAPPENED IN THIS ROOM.

BUT JAIRUS IS AN IMPORTANT MAN. NEWS ABOUT HIS DAUGHTER SPREADS QUICKLY. AND AS JESUS TRAVELS THROUGH GALILEE, PREACHING AND HEALING, HIS FAME INCREASED. THE PHARISEES WATCH ANGRILY. AS YET THEY HAVE NO REAL CASE AGAINST JESUS AND WITH- OUT ONE THEY DARE NOT STIR UP THE EXCITED CROWDS THAT FOLLOW HIM.

BUT JESUS IS CONCERNED ABOUT THE MANY PEOPLE WHO STILL HAVE NOT HEARD HIS MESSAGE. HE CALLS HIS DISCIPLES ASIDE.

THE PEOPLE ARE LIKE SHEEP WITHOUT A SHEPHERD. I WANT YOU TO GO OUT BY TWOS TO PREACH AND HEAL THE SICK AS I HAVE DONE. DO NOT BE WORRIED ABOUT WHAT TO SAY, FOR THE SPIRIT OF GOD WILL SPEAK THROUGH YOU.

THE DISCIPLES PREACH THROUGHOUT GALILEE. WHEN THEY RETURN JESUS PREPARES TO TAKE THEM TO A QUIET PLACE TO REST AND TALK ABOUT FUTURE PLANS. AS THEY ARE STARTING, A DISCIPLE OF JOHN THE BAPTIST BRINGS THEM TRAGIC NEWS.

JOHN HAS BEEN BEHEADED BY KING HEROD!

HEROD IS A WICKED MAN. BUT THIS IS THE WORST OF HIS SINS.

82

OUR BIBLE IN PICTURES
No Earthly Throne
FROM JOHN 6: 10-15; MATTHEW 14: 23-30

IT IS LATE AFTERNOON. THE CROWD THAT HAS FOLLOWED JESUS IS HUNGRY. BUT THE ONLY FOOD AVAILABLE BELONGS TO A BOY. HE EAGERLY GIVES IT TO JESUS, WHO THANKS GOD FOR IT AND HANDS IT TO HIS DISCIPLES.

DISTRIBUTE THE FOOD TO EVERYONE.

HOW FAR WILL FIVE LOAVES AND TWO FISHES GO IN FEEDING A CROWD OF OVER FIVE THOUSAND?

BUT THE DISCIPLES HAVE FAITH IN JESUS... AND THEY OBEY HIM.

LOOK! EVERYONE HERE IS GETTING ALL THE FOOD HE WANTS.

IT'S A MIRACLE!

WHEN THE PEOPLE HAVE FINISHED EATING, JESUS TURNS AGAIN TO HIS DISCIPLES.

GATHER UP THE FOOD THAT REMAINS.

TWELVE BASKETS OF FOOD ARE LEFT OVER! THE PEOPLE ARE NOW MORE AMAZED THAN EVER.

MAYBE JESUS IS THE KING THE PROPHETS TALKED ABOUT.

A KING LIKE DAVID -- WHO WILL DESTROY OUR ENEMIES AND MAKE US RICH AND POWERFUL!

UT GOD SENT JESUS TO BE THE SAVIOR, TO BRING MEN INTO THE KINGDOM OF GOD -- NOT TO COMMAND ARMIES AND CONQUER THRONES. WHEN JESUS SEES THAT THE CROWD WANTS TO FORCE HIM TO BE A KING, HE QUICKLY CALLS HIS DISCIPLES.

LAUNCH THE BOAT AND CROSS OVER TO THE OTHER SIDE OF THE SEA. I WILL JOIN YOU LATER.

QUICKLY -- BEFORE THE EXCITEMENT OF THE PEOPLE GROWS STRONGER -- JESUS DISMISSES THEM. THEN HE GOES UP ON A MOUNTAIN TO PRAY. LATER THAT NIGHT -- ON THE SEA OF GALILEE...

THE WIND IS RISING! WE'RE IN FOR A STORM!

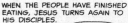

SOON THE STORM HITS...

HOW MUCH FARTHER TO LAND?

WE'RE ONLY HALF WAY.

SUDDENLY THEY LOOK UP TO SEE A FIGURE WALKING ON THE WATER. "A SPIRIT!" THEY CRY IN TERROR. ACROSS THE WAVES A CALM VOICE CALLS OUT: "IT IS I; DON'T BE AFRAID."

COME!

LORD! IF IT IS YOU, TELL ME TO COME TO YOU.

INSTANTLY PETER JUMPS FROM THE BOAT AND STARTS WALKING TOWARD JESUS. BUT WHEN HE SEES THE POWER OF THE WIND, HE LOSES FAITH-- AND BEGINS TO SINK...

OUR BIBLE IN PICTURES

Miracle on the Sea

FROM MATTHEW 14: 30-36; JOHN 6: 22-71; MARK 7:
1-23; MATTHEW 16: 13-26; 17: 1, 2

86

JESUS RESCUES PETER, AND AS THEY REACH THE BOAT, THE WIND DIES, AND THE SEA IS CALM.

ONLY SOMEONE FROM GOD COULD DO WHAT JESUS HAS DONE!

AT DAYBREAK THE DISCIPLES BRING THE BOAT TO SHORE. WHEN THE PEOPLE SEE JESUS, THEY HURRY TO BRING THEIR SICK AND CRIPPLED TO HIM. PATIENTLY AND LOVINGLY HE HEALS THEM ALL.

IF ONLY I CAN TOUCH HIS GARMENT I KNOW I WILL BE HEALED.

LATER THAT DAY JESUS GOES TO THE SYNAGOGUE IN CAPERNAUM. THE CROWD THAT HE FED THE DAY BEFORE IS THERE ASKING TO BE FED AGAIN. WHEN JESUS PREACHES A SERMON ABOUT THEIR SPIRITUAL NEEDS, MANY OF THEM ARE DISAPPOINTED AND TURN AWAY.

SEEING THIS, THE PHARISEES RESUME THEIR PUBLIC CRITICISM OF JESUS.

WE HAVE SEEN YOUR DISCIPLES EAT WITHOUT WASHING THEIR HANDS. WHY DO YOU LET THEM BREAK OUR LAWS AND DEFILE THEMSELVES?

NOTHING A MAN PUTS **INTO** HIS MOUTH CAN DEFILE HIM, BUT THE EVIL WORDS THAT COME **OUT** OF HIS MOUTH DEFILE HIM.

SHOCKED BECAUSE HE DEFENDS HIS DISCIPLES, THE PHARISEES TURN AWAY, MORE DETERMINED THAN EVER TO DESTROY JESUS.

DON'T YOU KNOW THAT YOU HAVE MADE THE PHARISEES ANGRY?

THE PHARISEES ARE BLIND TO THE WILL OF GOD—AND THEY ARE LEADING THE PEOPLE TO BE AS BLIND AS THEY ARE.

BECAUSE MOST OF THE PEOPLE WILL ACCEPT HIM ONLY AS AN EARTHLY KING, JESUS LEAVES GALILEE. HE TAKES HIS DISCIPLES TO THE COUNTRY OF PHENICIA—AND LATER TO THE REGION OF CAESAREA PHILIPPI, WHERE HE TEACHES THEM IN PRIVACY. THERE, ONE DAY, HE ASKS THEM: "WHO DO MEN SAY THAT I AM?"

JOHN THE BAPTIST... ELIJAH...

BUT WHO DO YOU SAY THAT I AM?

YOU ARE THE CHRIST, THE SON OF THE LIVING GOD.

BLESSED ARE YOU, PETER--FOR MY FATHER IN HEAVEN HAS REVEALED THIS TO YOU.

NOW THAT THE DISCIPLES TRULY UNDERSTAND THAT HE IS THE PROMISED MESSIAH, JESUS TELLS THEM WHAT WILL HAPPEN WHEN HE GOES TO JERUSALEM.

THE PHARISEES AND PRIESTS DO NOT BELIEVE THAT I AM THE MESSIAH. THEY WILL HAVE ME KILLED--BUT IN THREE DAYS I WILL RISE AGAIN.

89

A Boy—and His Father's Faith

FROM MATTHEW 17: 3-13; MARK 9: 33; LUKE 9: 37-45

ALONE WITH JESUS ON THE MOUNTAIN, PETER, JAMES AND JOHN SEE HIM TRANSFIGURED. HIS FACE SHINES WITH THE BRIGHTNESS OF THE SUN -- HIS CLOTHES BECOME DAZZLING WHITE. THEN TWO GREAT MEN OF THE PAST, MOSES AND ELIJAH, APPEAR TO TALK WITH HIM

BUT AS PETER SPEAKS A BRIGHT CLOUD DESCENDS ON THE MOUNTAINTOP... AND OUT OF THE CLOUD COMES THE VOICE OF GOD:

THIS IS MY BELOVED SON, IN WHOM I AM WELL PLEASED; HEAR YE HIM.

90

THE DISCIPLES ARE SO FRIGHTENED THAT THEY FALL TO THE GROUND BUT JESUS BENDS DOWN AND TOUCHES THEM...

DO NOT BE AFRAID.

THE NEXT MORNING -- ON THE WAY DOWN THE MOUNTAIN -- JESUS WARNS HIS DISCIPLES TO TELL NO ONE OF HIS TRANSFIGURATION UNTIL AFTER HIS RESURRECTION. AFTER WHAT THEY HAVE JUST SEEN THE DISCIPLES CANNOT BELIEVE THAT JESUS WILL DIE - SO THEY ARE PUZZLED WHEN JESUS TALKS ABOUT RISING FROM THE DEAD.

THEY REACH THE VALLEY TO FIND A GREAT CROWD GATHERED AROUND THE OTHER DISCIPLES.

AT THE SIGHT OF JESUS THE PEOPLE QUICKLY SURROUND HIM.

MY SON HAS SPELLS AND OFTEN FALLS INTO THE FIRE. I BROUGHT HIM TO YOUR DISCIPLES, BUT THEY COULD NOT HEAL HIM.

BRING YOUR SON TO ME.

THE FATHER OBEYS -- BUT THE BOY HAS A SPELL AND FALLS TO THE GROUND AT JESUS' FEET.

IF YOU CAN HELP US -- PLEASE DO.

ALL THINGS ARE POSSIBLE TO ONE WHO HAS FAITH.

I BELIEVE! HELP ME, PLEASE, TO HAVE MORE FAITH.

THOU UNCLEAN SPIRIT -- COME OUT OF THE BOY!

91

FOR A MOMENT THERE IS A STRUGGLE-- THEN THE BOY BECOMES SO STILL PEOPLE THINK HE IS DEAD. BUT JESUS REACHES DOWN TO TAKE HIS HAND.

ARISE!

INSTANTLY THE BOY GETS UP.

FATHER, WHAT HAPPENED?

YOU HAVE BEEN HEALED-- BY THE POWER OF GOD!

WHEN THEY ARE ALONE, THE DISCIPLES TURN TO JESUS.

WHY COULDN'T **WE** HEAL THE BOY?

YOU DID NOT HAVE FAITH. IF YOU HAVE FAITH THE SIZE OF A MUSTARD SEED, NOTHING IS IMPOSSIBLE FOR YOU.

LATER ON THE WAY TO CAPERNAUM, THE DISCIPLES TALK AMONG THEMSELVES ABOUT THE KINGDOM THEY EXPECT JESUS WILL SOON ESTABLISH. ALMOST AT ONCE THEY BEGIN TO QUARREL ABOUT WHICH ONE WILL BE THE GREATEST IN THAT KINGDOM.

IF ONLY **I** COULD SIT IN THE SEAT OF HONOR NEXT TO JESUS.

OUR BIBLE IN PICTURES

Seventy Times Seven

FROM MATTHEW 18: 1-14, 21, 22; JOHN 7: 11-52; 8: 21-59

ON THE WAY TO CAPERNAUM THE DISCIPLES QUARREL ABOUT WHICH ONE OF THEM WILL BE THE MOST IMPORTANT PERSON IN THE KINGDOM THEY EXPECT JESUS TO ESTABLISH. WHEN THEY REACH THE CITY JESUS ASKS WHY THEY ARE QUARRELING AND THEY ARE ASHAMED TO SAY. HE CALLS A LITTLE CHILD TO HIM.

WHICHEVER ONE OF YOU WANTS TO BE GREATEST IN GOD'S KINGDOM MUST BE AS HUMBLE AND WILLING TO LEARN AS THIS LITTLE CHILD.

94

WHEN THE CHIEF PRIESTS AND PHARISEES HEAR WHAT THE PEOPLE ARE SAYING, THEY QUICKLY JOIN FORCES AGAINST JESUS.

IF WE DON'T GET RID OF HIM THE PEOPLE WILL ACCEPT HIM AS THE MESSIAH.

I'LL STOP HIM. CALL THE TEMPLE GUARDS.

ARREST JESUS. BUT DO IT AT A TIME WHEN IT WILL CAUSE THE LEAST TROUBLE.

ON THE LAST DAY OF THE FEAST THE OFFICERS RETURN TO THE PRIESTS AND PHARISEES.

WHERE IS JESUS?

WE'VE NEVER HEARD ANYONE SPEAK AS THIS MAN DOES. WE COULD NOT ARREST HIM.

JESUS RETURNS TO THE TEMPLE TO PREACH. IN THE COURSE OF HIS SERMON HE NOT ONLY POINTS OUT THE SINS OF THE PRIESTS AND PHARISEES BUT DECLARES THAT HE WAS WITH GOD EVEN BEFORE THE DAYS OF THEIR GREAT FOREFATHER, ABRAHAM.

HOW DARE HE CLAIM SUCH RELATIONSHIP WITH GOD!

STONE HIM! STONE HIM!

THE PRIESTS AND PHARISEES ARE FURIOUS--BUT THEY ARE AFRAID TO FORCE THE ISSUE WHILE THE CITY IS FILLED WITH PEOPLE ATTENDING THE FEAST. BUT THE NEXT DAY...

95

The TEMPLE of JERUSALEM

In Jesus' time there was a huge, magnificent temple in Jerusalem. King Herod the Great built a few years before Christ was born. Parts of the temple were gleaming white marble overlaid in places with sheets of gold.

In this temple, Mary and Joseph found the boy Jesus listening to the priests and teachers and asking them very wise questions. (LUKE 2:46-52)

INSIDE THE TEMPLE WAS A SEPARATE, WALLED ENCLOSURE CALLED THE HOLY OF HOLIES. THIS WAS SHIELDED FROM EVERY-ONE BY A HEAVY VEIL. ONLY THE HIGH PRIEST COULD COME INTO THIS VERY HOLY PLACE. AT THE MOMENT JESUS DIED ON THE CROSS, THIS VEIL WAS TORN IN TWO BY THE HAND OF GOD. THIS MEANT THAT ANYONE WHO BELIEVED IN JESUS COULD ENTER GOD'S PRESENCE. (LUKE 23:45, MARK 15:38, MATT. 27:51)

WHEN WORSHIPERS CAME TO THE TEMPLE, THEY HAD TO BUY ANIMALS TO BE SACRIFICED TO GOD. SALE OF THESE SACRIFICES WAS CONTROLLED BY MERCHANTS WHOM THE PRIESTS APPOINTED. ANYBODY WHO WANTED TO MAKE MONEY OFFERINGS HAD TO EXCHANGE ORDINARY COINS FOR SPECIAL SHEKELS. THESE WERE SOLD BY MONEY-CHANGERS WHO WERE ALSO LICENSED BY THE TEMPLE PRIESTS.

JESUS CONDEMNED THIS PRACTICE AND DROVE THESE MERCHANTS AND MONEY-CHANGERS OUT OF THE TEMPLE, SAYING: "MY HOUSE SHALL BE CALLED THE HOUSE OF PRAYER; BUT YE HAVE MADE IT A DEN OF THIEVES." (MATTHEW 21:12,13)

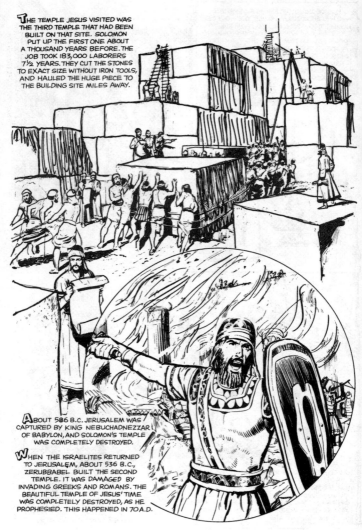

THE TEMPLE JESUS VISITED WAS THE THIRD TEMPLE THAT HAD BEEN BUILT ON THAT SITE. SOLOMON PUT UP THE FIRST ONE ABOUT A THOUSAND YEARS BEFORE. THE JOB TOOK 183,000 LABORERS 7½ YEARS. THEY CUT THE STONES TO EXACT SIZE WITHOUT IRON TOOLS, AND HAULED THE HUGE PIECE TO THE BUILDING SITE MILES AWAY.

ABOUT 586 B.C. JERUSALEM WAS CAPTURED BY KING NEBUCHADNEZZAR OF BABYLON, AND SOLOMON'S TEMPLE WAS COMPLETELY DESTROYED.

WHEN THE ISRAELITES RETURNED TO JERUSALEM, ABOUT 536 B.C., ZERUBBABEL BUILT THE SECOND TEMPLE. IT WAS DAMAGED BY INVADING GREEKS AND ROMANS. THE BEAUTIFUL TEMPLE OF JESUS' TIME WAS COMPLETELY DESTROYED, AS HE PROPHESIED. THIS HAPPENED IN 70 A.D.

A Jerusalem Beggar Meets the Son of God

FROM JOHN 9: 1—10: 21; LUKE 10: 25

THE PRIESTS AND PHARISEES ATTEMPT TO STONE JESUS -- BUT HE ESCAPES. LATER -- ON THE SABBATH -- HE AND HIS DISCIPLES COME UPON A BLIND MAN BEGGING AT A TEMPLE GATE. JESUS MOISTENS SOME CLAY AND PLACES IT TENDERLY OVER THE MAN'S EYES.

GO, WASH IN THE POOL OF SILOAM.

THE MAN OBEYS JESUS, AND FOR THE FIRST TIME IN HIS LIFE HE CAN SEE! HE IS SO EXCITED THAT HE HURRIES HOME, WHERE HE IS MET BY HIS NEIGHBORS.

IS THIS THE BLIND MAN WHO BEGGED OUTSIDE THE TEMPLE?

IMPOSSIBLE – BUT HE **DOES** LOOK LIKE HIM!

99

BUT **I AM** THE MAN WHO WAS BLIND. JESUS GAVE ME MY SIGHT!

THE NEIGHBORS ARE WORRIED BECAUSE THE MAN HAS BEEN HEALED ON THE SABBATH. THEY TAKE HIM AT ONCE TO THE PHARISEES, WHO INTERPRET THE RULES ABOUT WHAT CAN BE DONE ON THE SABBATH.

THIS JESUS YOU TALK ABOUT IS A SINNER -- HE DOESN'T OBEY THE LAWS OF THE SABBATH.

I DO NOT KNOW WHETHER HE IS A SINNER, BUT THIS I DO KNOW: I WAS BLIND AND NOW I SEE.

THE PHARISEES TRY TO MAKE THE MAN TURN AGAINST JESUS, BUT THEY CANNOT, SO THEY PUT HIM OUT OF THE SYNAGOGUE. JESUS LEARNS WHAT HAS HAPPENED, AND SEARCHES FOR THE THE MAN. WHEN HE FINDS HIM THE PHARISEES QUICKLY GATHER AROUND.

DO YOU BELIEVE IN THE SON OF GOD?

WHO IS HE-- THAT I MAY BELIEVE IN HIM?

I AM--THE VERY ONE WHO IS SPEAKING TO YOU.

LORD, I BELIEVE!

I AM THE GOOD SHEPHERD; THE GOOD SHEPHERD GIVES HIS LIFE FOR HIS SHEEP. NO ONE CAN TAKE MY LIFE FROM ME, BUT I GIVE IT MYSELF. I HAVE THE POWER TO GIVE IT AND TO TAKE IT AGAIN, FOR I RECEIVED THIS POWER FROM GOD MY FATHER.

THIS MAN IS CRAZY AND IS POSSESSED BY AN EVIL SPIRIT. WHY LISTEN TO HIM?

BUT CAN AN EVIL SPIRIT OPEN THE EYES OF THE BLIND?

WHILE JESUS IS PREACHING IN ONE OF THE CITIES A LAWYER IN THE CROWD WAITS FOR A CHANCE TO TEST HIM.

THE PHARISEES AND PRIESTS CONTINUE TO ARGUE. SOME THINK THAT JESUS IS WORKING WITH THE DEVIL. OTHERS DECLARE THAT HE IS NOT, BUT THEY REFUSE TO BELIEVE THAT HE IS THE SON OF GOD. A FEW DAYS LATER JESUS AND HIS DISCIPLES LEAVE JERUSALEM FOR A TOUR THROUGH JUDEA.

I'LL FIND OUT FOR MYSELF HOW THIS YOUNG TEACHER HANDLES A HARD QUESTION.

Four Travelers to Jericho

FROM LUKE 10: 25-39

ONE DAY WHILE JESUS IS PREACHING A LAWYER DECIDES TO TEST HIM. HE ASKS A QUESTION WHICH THE PHARISEES HAVE ANSWERED WITH A LOT OF COMPLICATED RULES.

WHAT SHALL I DO TO INHERIT ETERNAL LIFE?

JESUS REPLIES BY ASKING A QUESTION THAT FORCES THE LAWYER TO DISREGARD THE RULES OF THE PHARISEES AND GO STRAIGHT TO THE COMMANDMENTS OF GOD.

YOU ARE AN AUTHORITY ON GOD'S WORD -- WHAT DO HIS COMMANDMENTS SAY?

LOVE GOD WITH ALL THY HEART -- AND THY NEIGHBOR AS THYSELF.

YOU ARE RIGHT-- DO THAT AND YOU WILL HAVE ETERNAL LIFE.

BUT WHO IS MY NEIGHBOR?

JESUS REPLIES WITH A STORY WHICH FORCES THE LAWYER AGAIN TO ANSWER HIS OWN QUESTION:

A MAN IS TRAVELING FROM JERUSALEM TO JERICHO. ON THE WAY HE IS ATTACKED BY BANDITS, ROBBED, AND LEFT FOR DEAD.

BY CHANCE A PRIEST COMES BY-- HE SEES THE WOUNDED MAN BUT HE QUICKLY PASSES BY.

A LITTLE LATER A LEVITE, AN ASSISTANT TO THE PRIESTS, COMES ALONG-- BUT HE, TOO, HURRIES BY.

BUT WHEN A SAMARITAN SEES THE INJURED MAN, HE STOPS. ALTHOUGH SAMARITANS ARE BITTER ENEMIES OF THE JEWS, HE BINDS UP THE MAN'S WOUNDS, TAKES HIM TO AN INN, AND PAYS FOR HIS CARE.

WHEN HE FINISHES THE STORY OF THE GOOD SAMARITAN, JESUS ASKS: WHICH ONE OF THE THREE WAS A NEIGHBOR TO THE MAN WHO WAS ROBBED?

THE MAN WHO HELPED HIM.

GO AND DO THE SAME.

THE LAWYER GOES AWAY-- AMAZED AT THE SKILL WITH WHICH JESUS ANSWERED HIS QUESTIONS.

NOW I SEE-- MY NEIGHBOR IS ANYONE WHO NEEDS ME.

JESUS CONTINUES ON HIS PREACHING TOUR. IN BETHANY HE STOPS TO VISIT HIS FRIENDS: MARY, MARTHA, AND LAZARUS. MARY DROPS EVERYTHING SHE IS DOING TO LISTEN TO JESUS...

BUT HER SISTER MARTHA...

IT ISN'T FAIR-- AND I WON'T STAND FOR IT ANY LONGER!

104

The Lord's Prayer

FROM LUKE 10: 40—11: 2; MATTHEW 6: 9-13; JOHN 10: 22-40; LUKE 15: 1-19

WHEN JESUS VISITS IN THE HOME OF HIS FRIENDS, MARY, MARTHA, AND LAZARUS, MARY STOPS HER WORK TO LISTEN TO JESUS. BUT MARTHA HURRIES TO THE KITCHEN TO PREPARE FOOD. AS SHE WORKS SHE BECOMES UPSET BECAUSE MARY DOES NOT HELP HER. AT LAST SHE COMPLAINS TO JESUS.

DON'T YOU THINK IT'S WRONG FOR MARY TO LEAVE ME WITH ALL THE WORK TO DO? TELL HER TO HELP ME.

MARTHA! MARTHA! YOU ARE WORRYING ABOUT TOO MANY THINGS. ONLY ONE THING IS IMPORTANT --TO LEARN THE WILL OF GOD, AS MARY HAS CHOSEN TO DO.

DURING THE REST OF JESUS' VISIT, MARTHA SEEKS TO LEARN MORE ABOUT GOD. THEN JESUS LEAVES HIS FRIENDS IN BETHANY AND JOINS HIS DISCIPLES FOR A TEACHING TRIP IN JUDEA.

LISTENING TO JESUS MAKES ME FEEL SO CLOSE TO GOD.

DURING HIS TRAVELS JESUS STOPS OFTEN TO PRAY. HIS DISCIPLES SEE THE POWER OF PRAYER IN JESUS' LIFE, AND ONE DAY A DISCIPLE SPEAKS TO HIM ABOUT IT.

TEACH US TO PRAY.

JESUS ANSWERS: WHEN YOU PRAY, SAY,

OUR FATHER WHICH ART IN HEAVEN, HALLOWED BE THY NAME. THY KINGDOM COME. THY WILL BE DONE IN EARTH, AS IT IS IN HEAVEN. GIVE US THIS DAY OUR DAILY BREAD. AND FORGIVE US OUR DEBTS, AS WE FORGIVE OUR DEBTORS. AND LEAD US NOT INTO TEMPTATION, BUT DELIVER US FROM EVIL: FOR THINE IS THE KINGDOM, AND THE POWER, AND THE GLORY, FOR EVER. AMEN.

FOR A MOMENT NO ONE SPEAKS. THEN SOFTLY THE DISCIPLES SAY "AMEN" TO THE SIMPLE PRAYER THAT BECOMES A MODEL FOR THEIR FUTURE PRAYERS TO GOD. AFTER THIS, JESUS AND HIS HELPERS CONTINUE THROUGH JUDEA, PREACHING AND HEALING. BY THE TIME JESUS RETURNS TO JERUSALEM FOR A RELIGIOUS FEAST THE CITY IS FILLED WITH PEOPLE TALKING AND WONDERING ABOUT HIM.

AS JESUS IS WALKING ALONG SOLOMON'S PORCH OF THE TEMPLE, THE PEOPLE SURROUND HIM.

HOW LONG WILL YOU KEEP US WAITING? IF YOU ARE THE MESSIAH, TELL US.

I TOLD YOU, BUT YOU WOULD NOT BELIEVE ME. THE THINGS I HAVE DONE IN MY FATHER'S NAME SHOULD PROVE TO YOU WHO I AM.

DID YOU HEAR THAT? HE CALLED GOD HIS FATHER!

STONE HIM!

JESUS TURNS AND QUIETLY WALKS AWAY, AND--STRANGELY--NO ONE TRIES TO STOP HIM.

JESUS LEAVES JERUSALEM FOR PEREA--WHERE HE CONTINUES TO PREACH AND HEAL THE SICK. AGAIN THE PHARISEES COMPLAIN BECAUSE HE ASSOCIATES WITH SINNERS. JESUS TELLS THEM A STORY...

A CERTAIN MAN HAS TWO SONS. ONE DAY THE YOUNGER COMES TO HIM.

FATHER, I WANT TO RUN MY OWN LIFE. PLEASE GIVE ME THE SHARE OF YOUR MONEY THAT WILL SOMEDAY BE MINE.

I HAD HOPED YOU WOULD STAY HOME AND HELP WITH THE WORK HERE--BUT IF YOU WANT THE MONEY, YOU MAY HAVE IT.

THE YOUNG MAN GOES TO ANOTHER COUNTRY-- WHERE HE SPENDS HIS MONEY EATING AND DRINKING WITH BAD COMPANIONS. AT LAST HIS MONEY IS GONE--AND THE ONLY JOB HE CAN GET IS CARING FOR A FARMER'S PIGS.

MY FATHER'S SERVANTS LIVE BETTER THAN THIS! I'M GOING HOME AND ASK MY FATHER TO LET ME WORK FOR HIM--NOT AS HIS SON, BUT AS A SERVANT!

The Prodigal's Return

FROM LUKE 15: 20-32; JOHN 11: 1-8

WHEN THE PHARISEES COMPLAIN BECAUSE JESUS ASSOCIATES WITH SINNERS, HE TELLS THEM A STORY ABOUT A YOUNG MAN WHO LEAVES HOME. THE YOUNG MAN SPENDS HIS MONEY SO FOOLISHLY THAT AT LAST HE HAS TO TAKE CARE OF A FARMER'S PIGS IN ORDER TO KEEP ALIVE. IN HIS MISERY HE DECIDES TO GO HOME AND WORK FOR HIS FATHER-- NOT AS HIS SON, BUT AS ONE OF HIS SERVANTS. WHEN HE REACHES HOME HIS FATHER RUSHES OUT TO MEET HIM.

FATHER! I HAVE SINNED AGAINST HEAVEN AND YOU. I'M NO LONGER WORTHY TO BE CALLED YOUR SON.

BRING MY SON THE BEST ROBE IN THE HOUSE. AND PREPARE A FEAST, FOR MY SON WHO WAS LOST IS FOUND!

OUT IN THE FIELD THE OLDER SON WORKS HARD TO COMPLETE HIS JOB BEFORE NIGHT.

IF MY BROTHER WERE HERE TO HELP, I WOULDN'T HAVE TO WORK SO MUCH.

F DAY'S WORK DONE, HE GOES HOME. [AS] HE APPROACHES THE HOUSE HE [HE]ARS MUSIC...

WHAT'S GOING ON?

YOUR BROTHER HAS RETURNED, AND YOUR FATHER IS HAVING A FEAST FOR HIM.

IN ANGER THE OLDER SON REFUSES TO GO INTO THE HOUSE. SOON HIS FATHER COMES OUT.

YOU HAVE NEVER GIVEN A FEAST FOR ME ALTHOUGH I HAVE STAYED HOME TO HELP YOU, BUT MY BROTHER--

ALL THAT I HAVE IS YOURS, MY SON. BUT IT IS RIGHT FOR US TO BE GLAD FOR YOUR BROTHER'S RETURN. HE WAS THE SAME AS DEAD-- NOW HE IS ALIVE.

WHEN JESUS FINISHES THE STORY THE PEOPLE TURN TO ONE ANOTHER IN WONDER.

DOES HE MEAN THAT GOD IS LIKE THE FATHER IN THE STORY?

YES-- I SEE IT. GOD WANTS TO FORGIVE EVEN US SINNERS IF WE WILL COME BACK TO HIM.

WHEN THE PHARISEES SEE THE REACTION OF THE PEOPLE, THEY TURN AWAY IN ANGER. JESUS CONTINUES TO TEACH, BUT HE IS SOON INTERRUPTED...

JESUS! MARY AND MARTHA HAVE SENT ME TO TELL YOU THAT THEIR BROTHER, LAZARUS, IS ILL. THEY WANT YOU TO COME TO BETHANY--

BETHANY? THAT'S TOO CLOSE TO HIS ENEMIES IN JERUSALEM. THEY'LL KILL HIM!

Called from the Tomb

JOHN 11: 38-54; LUKE 18: 15-23; 19: 1-3

BY THE TIME JESUS AND HIS DISCIPLES REACH BETHANY LAZARUS, THE BROTHER OF MARY AND MARTHA, HAS BEEN DEAD FOUR DAYS. AT THE TOMB JESUS ASKS TO HAVE THE STONE ROLLED AWAY. HE PRAYS ALOUD TO GOD, AND THEN CALLS OUT IN A STRONG VOICE...

LAZARUS, COME FORTH.

111

TO THE AMAZEMENT OF THE CROWD, LAZARUS APPEARS!

LAZARUS!

O JESUS, WE THANK YOU!

A MAN RAISED FROM THE DEAD! THE PEOPLE CAN SCARCELY BELIEVE WHAT THEY HAVE SEEN. MANY OF THEM TURN TO JESUS CRYING, "MESSIAH! SON OF GOD!" BUT OTHERS GO INTO JERUSALEM TO TELL THE PHARISEES WHAT JESUS HAS DONE.

IN ANGER AND DESPERATION THE PHARISEES AND CHIEF PRIESTS CALL A MEETING.

IF NEWS OF THIS GETS AROUND THE PEOPLE WILL TRY TO MAKE JESUS A KING.

AND IF THERE'S A REBELLION THE ROMANS WILL BLAME US. WE'LL LOSE OUR POSITIONS AND THE NATION WILL BE DESTROYED.

DON'T YOU SEE? IT IS BETTER TO KILL JESUS THAN TO GET THE WHOLE COUNTRY IN TROUBLE.

CAIAPHAS IS A SHREWD ONE. HE'S FOUND A REASON TO KILL JESUS -- AND HE'LL ALSO FIND A WAY.

WHEN JESUS LEARNS OF THIS NEW PLOT AGAINST HIM, HE GOES OFF TO A QUIET PLACE -- TO WAIT UNTIL THE TIME COMES TO FACE HIS ENEMIES.

AS THE TIME FOR THE PASSOVER FEAST APPROACHES, PEOPLE FROM ALL OVER PALESTINE SET OUT FOR JERUSALEM -- AND JESUS JOINS THEM.

ON THE WAY THE CROWDS BEG TO SEE AND HEAR JESUS.

NO -- NO -- TAKE YOUR CHILDREN AWAY. JESUS IS TOO BUSY --

BUT I WANT JESUS TO BLESS MY LITTLE SON.

LET THE LITTLE ONES COME TO ME -- FOR GOD'S KINGDOM IS MADE UP OF PEOPLE WITH LOVE AND TRUST SUCH AS THEIRS.

FARTHER ALONG THE WAY JESUS IS STOPPED BY A YOUNG MAN.

TEACHER, WHAT SHALL I DO TO INHERIT ETERNAL LIFE?

KEEP GOD'S COMMANDMENTS.

BUT I HAVE KEPT THE LAWS -- SINCE I WAS A BOY.

YOU NEED TO DO ONE THING MORE -- SELL ALL THAT YOU HAVE, GIVE THE MONEY TO THE POOR, AND FOLLOW ME.

BUT THE YOUNG MAN THINKS TOO MUCH OF HIS RICHES... SLOWLY HE TURNS HIS BACK ON JESUS AND WALKS AWAY.

THE TRAVELERS CONTINUE ON TOWARD JERUSALEM. BY THE TIME THEY REACH JERICHO, JESUS IS IN THE MIDST OF AN EXCITED, HAPPY THRONG.

PLEASE --LET ME THROUGH!

HO -- ZACCHEUS, THE CROOKED LITTLE TAX COLLECTOR, WANTS TO SEE JESUS!

I HAVE TO SEE JESUS -- AND I WILL!

Man in the Tree

FROM LUKE 19: 4-10; JOHN 12: 1-8; LUKE 19: 29-35

ZACCHEUS, THE WEALTHY TAX COLLECTOR,
IS SO SHORT THAT HE CAN'T LOOK
OVER THE HEADS OF THE PEOPLE. FRANTICALLY
HE RUNS AHEAD OF THE CROWD, CLIMBS A TREE,
AND WAITS. WHEN JESUS
SEES HIM, HE STOPS...

ZACCHEUS, COME DOWN, FOR I WANT TO STAY AT YOUR HOUSE!

ZACCHEUS IS AMAZED THAT JESUS WOULD EVEN SPEAK TO HIM, BUT HE CLIMBS DOWN AT ONCE AND LEADS THE WAY TO HIS HOUSE.

WHY WOULD A TEACHER AS GREAT AS JESUS WANT TO STAY WITH THAT CROOKED LITTLE TAX COLLECTOR?

ZACCHEUS WONDERS, TOO, BUT HE SOON DISCOVERS THAT BEING IN THE PRESENCE OF JESUS MAKES HIM ASHAMED OF EVERY WRONG THING HE HAS EVER DONE. HE WANTS TO BE FORGIVEN AND START OVER..

HALF OF MY GOODS I WILL GIVE TO THE POOR. AND IF I HAVE CHEATED ANYONE I WILL PAY HIM BACK FOUR TIMES AS MUCH.

SALVATION HAS COME TO YOU TODAY, ZACCHEUS. IT IS TO HELP PEOPLE LIKE YOU THAT I HAVE COME TO THE WORLD.

FROM JERICHO THE CROWDS CONTINUE THEIR WAY TO JERUSALEM FOR THE GREAT PASSOVER FEAST. THE FESTIVAL IS STILL SIX DAYS AWAY, SO JESUS STOPS IN BETHANY TO VISIT HIS FRIENDS-- MARY, MARTHA, AND LAZARUS. AT A SUPPER IN THE HOME OF SIMON THE LEPER, MARY KNEELS BESIDE JESUS AND ANOINTS HIS FEET WITH COSTLY OIL--THEN WIPES THEM WITH HER HAIR.

JUDAS ISCARIOT, TREASURER OF THE DISCIPLES, IS ANGERED BY WHAT HE THINKS IS A WASTE OF MONEY.

WHY WASN'T THE OIL SOLD AND THE MONEY GIVEN TO THE POOR?

I WANTED TO HONOR JESUS--

LET HER ALONE. SHE IS SHOWING HER LOVE FOR ME.

JUDAS IS ANGERED BY THIS REPRIMAND-- AND AN UGLY THOUGHT COMES TO HIS MIND.

WHEN THE TIME IS RIGHT I'LL GO TO THE PRIESTS AND PHARISEES-- **THEY'LL** BE GLAD TO LISTEN TO ME.

THE NEXT DAY JESUS AND HIS DISCIPLES JOIN THE CROWDS GOING UP TO JERUSALEM TO PREPARE FOR THE PASSOVER FEAST. ON THE WAY...

GO OVER INTO THAT VILLAGE AND AS YOU ENTER YOU WILL FIND A COLT. BRING IT TO ME. AND IF ANYONE QUESTIONS YOU, TELL HIM I NEED THE ANIMAL-- AND WILL RETURN IT.

PUZZLED, THE TWO DISCIPLES GO TO THE VILLAGE WHERE THEY FIND THE COLT. WHEN THEY START TO UNTIE THE ROPE...

WHAT DO YOU MEAN, TAKING MY ANIMAL?

JESUS SAID TO TELL YOU THAT HE NEEDED IT.

AT THE MENTION OF JESUS' NAME, THE MAN GLADLY GIVES HIS CONSENT.

I WONDER WHY JESUS WANTS MY COLT. IT HAS NEVER BEEN RIDDEN-- BESIDES, IT'S NOT A VERY NOBLE BEAST FOR ANYONE AS IMPORTANT AS JESUS TO RIDE.

Triumphal Entry

LUKE 19: 36-38; MATTHEW 21: 10-17

IT IS THE FIRST DAY OF THE WEEK. THE ROAD TO JERUSALEM IS FILLED WITH PEOPLE ON THE WAY TO CELEBRATE THE PASSOVER FEAST OF THE JEWS. AT JESUS' REQUEST HIS DISCIPLES BRING HIM A LOWLY BEAST OF BURDEN—HE MOUNTS IT AND JOINS THE MULTITUDE OF PILGRIMS. EAGERLY THEY MAKE WAY FOR HIM—WAVING PALM BRANCHES AND CARPETING HIS PATH WITH THEIR GARMENTS. AND, WHILE THEY ESCORT HIM—TRIUMPHANTLY—UP THE ROAD AND INTO THE CITY, THE SOUND OF THEIR PRAISES FILLS THE AIR: "HOSANNA! BLESSED IS THE KING THAT COMETH IN THE NAME OF THE LORD!"

119

120

WHEN JESUS BEGINS TO PREACH, PEOPLE CROWD INTO THE TEMPLE COURTS TO HEAR HIM. BUT BEHIND CLOSED DOORS THE PRIESTS AND PHARISEES PLOT THEIR STRATEGY. BY TUESDAY THEY ARE READY...

The Great Commandment

FROM LUKE 20: 23-26; MARK 12: 28-34, 38-44; 13;
MATTHEW 26: 14-16

Jesus IS PREACHING IN A COURT OF THE TEMPLE, AND IN AN ATTEMPT TO GET HIM INTO TROUBLE, THE PHARISEES ASK: "IS IT RIGHT TO PAY TAXES TO CAESAR?" JESUS KNOWS THAT THIS IS A TRICK QUESTION. IF HE ANSWERS "YES," THE PEOPLE WILL TURN AGAINST HIM. IF HE SAYS "NO," THE ROMANS WILL ARREST HIM FOR TREASON. HE ASKS TO SEE A ROMAN COIN.

WHOSE IMAGE IS THIS?

CAESAR'S.

QUIETLY JESUS RETURNS THE COIN.

GIVE TO CAESAR THE THINGS THAT ARE HIS, AND TO GOD THE THINGS THAT ARE GOD'S.

THE PHARISEES ARE ANGRY AT BEING DEFEATED AGAIN, BUT THEY MARVEL AT JESUS' SKILL IN HANDLING THEIR TRICK QUESTION. LATER IN THE DAY ONE OF THEM ASKS ANOTHER DIFFICULT QUESTION.

WHICH OF OUR 613 COMMANDMENTS IS THE MOST IMPORTANT?

THOU SHALT LOVE THE LORD THY GOD WITH ALL THY HEART, AND WITH ALL THY SOUL, AND WITH ALL THY MIND, AND WITH ALL THY STRENGTH. AND THE SECOND IS THIS: THOU SHALT LOVE THY NEIGHBOR AS THYSELF.

YOU HAVE SPOKEN THE TRUTH. TO LOVE GOD AND ONE'S NEIGHBOR IS MORE IMPORTANT THAN ALL BURNT OFFERINGS.

YOU ARE NOT FAR FROM THE KINGDOM OF GOD.

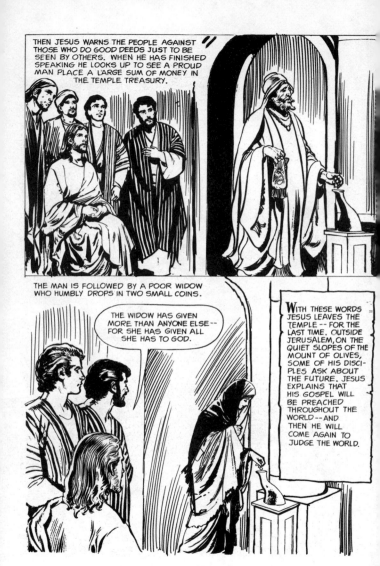

THEN JESUS WARNS THE PEOPLE AGAINST THOSE WHO DO GOOD DEEDS JUST TO BE SEEN BY OTHERS. WHEN HE HAS FINISHED SPEAKING HE LOOKS UP TO SEE A PROUD MAN PLACE A LARGE SUM OF MONEY IN THE TEMPLE TREASURY.

THE MAN IS FOLLOWED BY A POOR WIDOW WHO HUMBLY DROPS IN TWO SMALL COINS.

THE WIDOW HAS GIVEN MORE THAN ANYONE ELSE-- FOR SHE HAS GIVEN ALL SHE HAS TO GOD.

WITH THESE WORDS JESUS LEAVES THE TEMPLE -- FOR THE LAST TIME. OUTSIDE JERUSALEM, ON THE QUIET SLOPES OF THE MOUNT OF OLIVES, SOME OF HIS DISCIPLES ASK ABOUT THE FUTURE. JESUS EXPLAINS THAT HIS GOSPEL WILL BE PREACHED THROUGHOUT THE WORLD-- AND THEN HE WILL COME AGAIN TO JUDGE THE WORLD.

I WANT TO SEE THE CHIEF PRIEST.

A MAN NAMED JUDAS ISCARIOT WANTS TO SEE YOU. HE SAYS IT'S URGENT.

JUDAS ISCARIOT? WHY, HE'S ONE OF JESUS' DISCIPLES. SHOW HIM IN.

I KNOW HOW MUCH YOU WANT TO GET RID OF JESUS. WHAT WILL YOU GIVE TO HAVE HIM DELIVERED TO YOU -- AWAY FROM THE CROWDS THAT BELIEVE IN HIM?

THIRTY PIECES OF SILVER.

Secretly—in an Upper Room

FROM LUKE 22: 7-13; JOHN 13: 1-20, 27-30; MATTHEW 26: 21-25

IT IS LATE TUESDAY NIGHT WHEN JUDAS BARGAINS WITH THE CHIEF PRIESTS TO BETRAY JESUS. AFTER THE AGREEMENT IS MADE HE RETURNS TO BETHANY AND SPENDS WEDNESDAY WITH JESUS AND THE DISCIPLES-- NEVER SUSPECTING THAT JESUS KNOWS WHAT HE HAS DONE. THURSDAY, JESUS CALLS PETER AND JOHN ASIDE.

GO INTO JERUSALEM AND MAKE THINGS READY FOR THE PASSOVER FEAST.

WHERE CAN WE GO SO THAT YOUR ENEMIES WILL NOT SEE US?

WHEN YOU ENTER THE CITY YOU WILL SEE A MAN CARRYING A PITCHER. FOLLOW HIM AND ASK HIS MASTER TO SHOW YOU THE ROOM THAT WE MAY USE.

PETER AND JOHN GO AT ONCE TO JERUSALEM. THEY FIND THE SERVANT CARRYING A PITCHER AND FOLLOW HIM HOME.

WHERE IS THE ROOM IN WHICH JESUS AND HIS DISCIPLES CAN EAT THE PASSOVER?

COME WITH ME.

THE MAN LEADS THEM QUICKLY UP THE STAIRS TO A BIG UPPER ROOM.

I'M HONORED TO HAVE JESUS CELEBRATE THE PASSOVER IN MY HOUSE.

PETER AND JOHN PREPARE FOR THE FEAST, AND THAT EVENING JESUS JOINS THE TWELVE IN THE UPPER ROOM. AFTER THEY ARE SEATED JESUS KNEELS, LIKE A SERVANT, TO WASH THE FEET OF HIS DISCIPLES.

NO, LORD. I'M NOT GOOD ENOUGH TO HAVE **YOU** WAIT ON ME!

IF YOU DO NOT LET ME SERVE YOU, PETER, YOU WILL HAVE NO PLACE IN MY KINGDOM.

127

AFTER JESUS HAS WASHED ALL OF THE DISCIPLES' FEET, HE SITS DOWN AT THE TABLE AGAIN.

IF I, YOUR LORD AND MASTER, HAVE SERVED YOU, YOU SHOULD DO THE SAME FOR ONE ANOTHER. THE SERVANT IS NOT GREATER THAN HIS MASTER.

AFTER A FEW MINUTES JESUS MAKES A STARTLING STATEMENT.

ONE OF YOU IS GOING TO BETRAY ME.

BETRAY YOU? IS IT I, LORD?

JESUS REPLIES THAT IT IS ONE WHO IS EATING WITH HIM NOW. JUDAS LEANS FORWARD.

IS IT I?

YOU HAVE SAID IT. WHAT YOU ARE GOING TO DO, JUDAS, DO QUICKLY.

AT ONCE THE TRAITOR RISES FROM THE TABLE AND HURRIES AWAY. BUT THE OTHER DISCIPLES DO NOT UNDERSTAND WHY...

The Lord's Supper

FROM LUKE 22: 17-20; JOHN 13: 33-38; 14; MATTHEW 26: 30, 36-56

129

IN A LITTLE WHILE I MUST LEAVE YOU. YOU CANNOT FOLLOW ME, BUT BEFORE I GO, LET ME REMIND YOU: LOVE ONE ANOTHER AS I HAVE LOVED YOU.

LORD, WHY CAN'T I FOLLOW YOU? YOU KNOW I'D GIVE MY LIFE FOR YOU.

PETER, BEFORE THE COCK CROWS YOU WILL DENY ME THREE TIMES.

DENY MY LORD? NEVER! MY SWORD IS READY THIS MINUTE FOR THE FIRST PERSON WHO TRIES TO HARM HIM.

THE DISCIPLES ARE FRIGHTENED AT THE THOUGHT OF JESUS LEAVING THEM.

DO NOT BE AFRAID. BELIEVE IN GOD; BELIEVE ALSO IN ME. IF YOU LOVE ME, KEEP MY COMMANDMENTS, AND I WILL ASK GOD TO SEND YOU THE HOLY SPIRIT TO COMFORT YOU. HE WILL BE WITH YOU FOREVER. COME, IT IS TIME TO GO...

QUIETLY, THEY LEAVE THE UPPER ROOM. THEY WALK THROUGH THE MOONLIT STREETS OF THE CITY, OUT AN EAST GATE, AND ACROSS A VALLEY TO THE GARDEN OF GETHSEMANE ON THE MOUNT OF OLIVES.

AT THE ENTRANCE JESUS ASKS EIGHT OF THE DISCIPLES TO WAIT WHILE HE TAKES HIS CLOSEST DISCIPLES, PETER, JAMES, AND JOHN FARTHER INTO THE GARDEN.

THIS IS A SAD NIGHT FOR ME -- STAY HERE AND WATCH WHILE I GO ALONE TO PRAY.

O MY FATHER, IF THOU BE WILLING, REMOVE THIS AGONY FROM ME; NEVERTHELESS NOT MY WILL, BUT THINE BE DONE.

WHEN JESUS RETURNS TO HIS DISCIPLES, HE FINDS THEM SLEEPING. TWO MORE TIMES HE GOES ASIDE TO PRAY, AND EACH TIME HE FINDS HIS FRIENDS ASLEEP. AFTER WAKING THEM THE THIRD TIME...

ARISE -- THE ONE WHO IS TO BETRAY ME IS NEAR.

AS JESUS SPEAKS, JUDAS LEADS A BAND OF MEN INTO THE GARDEN. ACCORDING TO HIS AGREEMENT, HE IDENTIFIES JESUS WITH A KISS.

GREETINGS, MASTER!

AS THE SOLDIERS TAKE HOLD OF JESUS, PETER DRAWS HIS SWORD. SLASHING WILDLY, HE CUTS OFF THE EAR OF A SERVANT.

PETER, PUT UP YOUR SWORD. DO YOU THINK THAT I CANNOT CALL ON GOD TO SEND LEGIONS OF ANGELS TO PROTECT ME?

QUIETLY JESUS HEALS THE MAN'S EAR. WHEN THE DISCIPLES SEE THAT JESUS IS MAKING NO ATTEMPT TO SAVE HIMSELF, THEY RUN FOR THEIR LIVES. AT AN OFFICER'S COMMAND, THE SOLDIERS BIND JESUS AND TAKE HIM BACK TO JERUSALEM -- THE CITY INTO WHICH HE HAD RIDDEN SO TRIUMPHANTLY ONLY A FEW DAYS BEFORE!

BY THE LIGHT OF A
TORCH

THE PEOPLE WHO LIVED IN JESUS' DAY DID NOT LIKE TO STAY OUTSIDE AFTER DARK. SOME STREETS HAD OIL LAMPS, BUT THESE GAVE VERY FEEBLE LIGHT AND SIDE STREETS WERE DARK. SO TORCHES OR SMALL OIL LAMPS WERE ALWAYS USED TO LIGHT THE WAY AT NIGHT. BECAUSE LAMPS WERE FAMILIAR TO EVERYONE, JESUS USED A STORY ABOUT A LAMP TO EXPLAIN HOW PEOPLE SHOULD BE PREPARED FOR THE LORD'S COMING.

MOST HOMES WHERE JESUS STAYED WERE POORLY LIGHTED. OIL LAMPS WERE HUNG FROM THE CEILING BY CHAINS, OR SET ON SMALL SHELVES AND LAMP STANDS.

TORCHES WERE USUALLY MADE OF STICKS OR TWIGS TIED TOGETHER WITH TWINE, AND STUFFED WITH GRASS THAT HAD BEEN SOAKED IN BURNABLE RESIN, PITCH OR OIL.

THERE WERE NO MATCHES OR GAS BURNERS, AND FIRES WERE DIFFICULT TO LIGHT WITH FLINT, STEEL AND TINDER...SO THE HOME FIRES WERE ALWAYS KEPT BURNING. IF THE FIRE IN A HOUSE DIED OUT, LIVE COALS WERE BORROWED FROM A NEIGHBOR.

THE CLAY LAMPS USED IN HOUSES WERE FILLED WITH OLIVE OIL.

JOHN 18:3 TELLS HOW JUDAS LED SOLDIERS CARRYING TORCHES AND LANTERNS TO THE GARDEN OF GETHSEMANE, WHERE THEY FOUND JESUS PRAYING.

Tried—and Denied!

FROM MATTHEW 26: 57-75; JOHN 18: 28-38; LUKE 23: 6-12

FOLLOWING HIS ARREST, JESUS IS BROUGHT TO THE PALACE OF THE HIGH PRIEST. FALSE WITNESSES BOLDLY ACCUSE HIM OF MANY THINGS --BUT THEY CAN PROVE NOTHING. FINALLY THE HIGH PRIEST QUESTIONS THE PRISONER.

ARE YOU THE CHRIST, THE SON OF GOD?

I AM.

THERE! YOU HEARD HIM. ANYONE WHO SPEAKS BLASPHEMY BY CLAIMING TO BE GOD'S SON DESERVES TO DIE.

INSTANTLY THE GUARDS TURN ON JESUS --SPITTING ON HIM, COVERING HIS FACE AND DEMANDING THAT HE PROVE HIS POWER BY IDENTIFYING THOSE WHO STRIKE HIM.

WHILE JESUS IS SUFFERING THESE INSULTS, PETER -- WHO HAS SECRETLY FOLLOWED HIM INTO THE CITY -- WARMS HIS HANDS BY A FIRE IN THE PALACE COURTYARD. WHILE HE IS TALKING, A MAID STOPS AND LOOKS AT HIM...

YOU WERE ONE OF THOSE WITH JESUS OF NAZARETH.

ME? I DON'T KNOW WHAT YOU'RE TALKING ABOUT.

AFRAID OF BEING QUESTIONED FURTHER, PETER GOES OUT INTO THE HALLWAY, BUT THERE...

THIS FELLOW WAS WITH JESUS.

JESUS? I DON'T EVEN KNOW THE MAN.

ABOUT AN HOUR LATER SOME MEN APPROACH PETER.

DIDN'T I SEE YOU IN THE GARDEN WHEN THE SOLDIERS TOOK JESUS?

YOU ARE A GALILEAN LIKE JESUS. I CAN TELL BY THE WAY YOU TALK.

FOR THE THIRD TIME PETER DENIES KNOWING JESUS-- AND THEN THE COCK CROWS! STARTLED, PETER RAISES HIS HEAD--TO LOOK STRAIGHT INTO THE EYES OF JESUS, WHO IS BEING LED OUT OF THE COURT.

SICK WITH SHAME, PETER RUSHES OUTSIDE, WEEPING BITTERLY.

THREE TIMES I DENIED MY LORD--JUST AS HE SAID I WOULD! O GOD, FORGIVE ME, FORGIVE ME!

IN THE EARLY HOURS OF FRIDAY MORNING THE MEMBERS OF THE JEWISH HIGH COURT, WHICH CANNOT SENTENCE A MAN TO DEATH, TAKE JESUS TO THE ROMAN GOVERNOR, PILATE. CLEVERLY, THEY CHARGE HIM-- NOT WITH BREAKING JEWISH LAWS -- BUT WITH TREASON AGAINST ROME. PILATE QUESTIONS JESUS PRIVATELY AND THEN RETURNS HIM TO THE PRIESTS AND CROWDS THAT HAVE GATHERED OUTSIDE.

I DO NOT FIND THIS MAN GUILTY OF ANY CRIME.

NOT GUILTY? WHY, HE TRIED TO START REVOLTS ALL OVER JUDEA AND GALILEE!

AT THE MENTION OF GALILEE, PILATE SENDS JESUS TO HEROD, THE RULER OF GALILEE, WHO IS IN JERUSALEM FOR THE PASSOVER. HEROD IS CURIOUS AND ASKS JESUS TO PERFORM SOME MIRACLE. WHEN JESUS WILL NOT, HEROD AND HIS SOLDIERS MAKE FUN OF HIM--AND THEN RETURN HIM TO PILATE.

PILATE IS TRAPPED. HE DOES NOT BELIEVE JESUS IS GUILTY OF TREASON. "BUT, IF I LET HIM GO," HE ARGUES TO HIMSELF, "AND THE JEWISH LEADERS MAKE TROUBLE, THE EMPEROR IN ROME WILL HOLD ME RESPONSIBLE." FINALLY HE THINKS OF A WAY TO EASE HIS CONSCIENCE AND PROTECT HIMSELF...

THE PEOPLE! I'LL LET THEM DECIDE!

138

PILATE IS STUNNED. HE MAKES ANOTHER ATTEMPT TO SAVE JESUS.

SCOURGE HIM.

MAYBE THE PEOPLE WILL BE SATISFIED IF THE PRISONER IS PUNISHED.

SO JESUS IS WHIPPED WITH LEATHER THONGS. THEN, IN SPORT, THE SOLDIERS MAKE A CROWN OF THORNS AND PLACE IT ON HIS HEAD.

HAIL, THE KING OF THE JEWS!

HOPING THE SIGHT OF JESUS, BRUTALLY BEATEN, WILL AROUSE THE CROWD'S SYMPATHY, PILATE PRESENTS HIM TO THE MULTITUDE.

BEHOLD THE MAN!

CRUCIFY HIM!

CRUCIFY HIM!

140

By this time even Pilate is sickened at the sight of such hate. But, not willing to endanger his position further, he surrenders Jesus to be crucified. As he does so he writes an inscription to be placed on Jesus' cross.

JESUS OF NAZARETH, THE KING OF THE JEWS.

It is Pilate's revenge. He knows that the Jewish leaders will burn with rage to see those words on the cross of a man they have condemned to die.

NO! NO! DON'T WRITE THAT HE IS THE KING OF THE JEWS. WRITE THAT HE SAID, "I AM KING OF THE JEWS."

WHAT I HAVE WRITTEN, I HAVE WRITTEN.

To Jesus, the hours from the time he was arrested until he is sentenced to be crucified have been filled with agony.

Sometime during those dark hours the traitor, Judas, realizes what he has done and rushes to the chief priests.

I HAVE SINNED-- I HAVE BETRAYED AN INNOCENT MAN.

WHAT IS THAT TO US?

HERE-- TAKE IT. I WANT NO PART OF YOUR DIRTY MONEY.

DRIVEN BY GUILT TOO GREAT TO BEAR, JUDAS GOES OUT AND HANGS HIMSELF.

BUT RETURNING THE MONEY DOES NOT SAVE THE MAN HE HAS BETRAYED. JESUS IS NOW IN THE HANDS OF THE ROMAN SOLDIERS-- WHO PLACE A HEAVY CROSS ON HIS BACK AND FORCE HIM OUT INTO THE STREET THAT LEADS TO A HILL CALLED CALVARY...

A King Is Crucified

FROM LUKE 23: 26-46; JOHN 19: 25-27

HAPPY, EXCITED PILGRIMS FROM ALL OVER PALESTINE HAVE BEEN CROWDING INTO JERUSALEM FOR DAYS TO CELEBRATE THE PASSOVER FEAST. BUT ON FRIDAY MORNING STARTLING NEWS SWEEPS ACROSS THE CITY LIKE A CHILLING WIND: JESUS OF NAZARETH IS GOING TO BE CRUCIFIED -- FOR TREASON!

THE STREET THAT LEADS TO THE HILL OF EXECUTION IS SOON FILLED WITH A STRANGE MIXTURE OF PEOPLE-- PRIESTS AND PHARISEES WHO DEMAND JESUS' DEATH; WOMEN WEEPING FOR THE MAN WHO FORGAVE SINS AND HEALED THE SICK; AND THE CURIOUS WHO WANT ONLY TO SEE A CONDEMNED MAN CARRY HIS CROSS...

ON THE WAY JESUS FALLS UNDER THE WEIGHT OF THE HEAVY CROSS. TO KEEP THE UGLY PROCESSION MOVING, THE ROMAN OFFICER SEIZES A BYSTANDER, SIMON FROM CYRENE.

HERE-- YOU CARRY THIS CROSS!

IT IS ABOUT NINE O'CLOCK WHEN JESUS, AND TWO ROBBERS WHO ARE TO BE CRUCIFIED WITH HIM, REACH CALVARY. AND THERE THE SON OF GOD IS NAILED TO A CROSS. ABOVE HIS HEAD IS FASTENED A SIGN: JESUS OF NAZARETH, THE KING OF THE JEWS!

FATHER, FORGIVE THEM: FOR THEY KNOW NOT WHAT THEY DO.

146

The Sealed Tomb

MARK 15: 38, 39; LUKE 23: 48, 49; JOHN 19: 38-42;
MATTHEW 27: 62-66

ABOUT NINE O'CLOCK FRIDAY MORNING JESUS OF NAZARETH IS CRUCIFIED OUTSIDE THE WALLS OF JERUSALEM. FROM NOON UNTIL THREE O'CLOCK DARKNESS COVERS THE LAND. THEN -- SUDDENLY -- AN EARTHQUAKE ROCKS THE GROUND. AND IN JERUSALEM...

THE VEIL BEFORE THE HOLIEST PLACE IN THE TEMPLE HAS BEEN RIPPED! WHAT CAN IT MEAN?

THE ANSWER IS THAT ON A HILL CALLED CALVARY THE SON OF GOD HAS GIVEN HIS LIFE TO PAY FOR THE SINS OF THE WORLD. THE VEIL IN THE TEMPLE NO LONGER SEPARATES MAN FROM THE PRESENCE OF GOD, FOR JESUS, THE SON, HAS OPENED THE WAY TO GOD, THE FATHER.

OUTSIDE THE CITY, EVEN THE ROMAN OFFICER WHO DIRECTED THE CRUCIFIXION IS AWED BY WHAT HAS HAPPENED. REVERENTLY, HE LOOKS UP AT THE MAN WHO FORGAVE HIS ENEMIES.

TRULY THIS MAN WAS GOD'S SON!

THE PEOPLE, TOO, ARE SHAKEN BY THE EXECUTION. AS THEY TURN BACK TO THE CITY...

I HAD HOPED THAT HE WAS THE ONE WHO WOULD DELIVER US FROM THE ROMANS.

IN JERUSALEM JOSEPH OF ARIMATHEA, A MEMBER OF THE JEWISH HIGH COURT AND SECRETLY A FOLLOWER OF JESUS, GOES BOLDLY TO PILATE.

MAY I HAVE THE BODY OF JESUS SO THAT WE MAY BURY IT BEFORE THE SABBATH?

YES... I'LL GIVE ORDERS TO MY OFFICER IN CHARGE.

REVERENTLY, JOSEPH TAKES THE BODY OF JESUS FROM THE CROSS. THEN HE AND HIS FRIEND, NICODEMUS, WRAP IT IN LINEN CLOTH, AND PLACE IT IN JOSEPH'S GARDEN TOMB.

EARLY THE NEXT DAY THE PRIESTS AND PHARISEES ALSO GO TO PILATE...

WE REMEMBER JESUS SAID THAT AFTER THREE DAYS HE WOULD RISE FROM THE DEAD. ORDER YOUR SOLDIERS TO SEAL AND GUARD THE TOMB SO THAT HIS DISCIPLES CAN'T STEAL THE BODY AND CLAIM THAT JESUS MADE GOOD ON HIS BOAST.

TAKE THE SOLDIERS YOU NEED AND SET UP A GUARD UNTIL AFTER THE THIRD DAY.

SO THE TOMB IS SEALED, AND ROMAN SOLDIERS ARE PLACED ON GUARD.

THERE-- THAT'S THE LAST WE'LL HEAR OF THIS MAN WHO CALLED HIMSELF THE SON OF GOD!

The Lord Is Risen

FROM MARK 16: 1-7; JOHN 20: 2-18; MATTHEW 28:
11-15; LUKE 24: 13-32

FRIDAY -- JUST OUTSIDE JERUSALEM -- JESUS OF NAZARETH IS CRUCIFIED AND BURIED. AT THE REQUEST OF THE PRIESTS AND PHARISEES, THE TOMB IS SEALED AND ROMAN SOLDIERS SET TO GUARD IT.

BUT ON THE MORNING OF THE THIRD DAY THE EARTH TREMBLES. AN ANGEL OF THE LORD DESCENDS -- AND ROLLS THE HEAVY STONE ASIDE. TERRIFIED, THE SOLDIERS FALL TO THE GROUND. WHEN THEY CAN GET TO THEIR FEET THEY RUSH BACK TO THE CITY.

THAT SAME MORNING MARY MAGDALENE AND OTHER FRIENDS OF JESUS HURRY TO THE TOMB WITH SPICES TO ANOINT HIS BODY. ON THE WAY, THEY WORRY ABOUT HOW THEY WILL GET THE STONE ROLLED AWAY. BUT WHEN THEY REACH THE GARDEN...

THE TOMB! IT IS OPEN!

BELIEVING THAT SOMEONE HAS STOLEN JESUS' BODY, MARY RUNS BACK TO JERUSALEM TO TELL PETER AND JOHN. BUT THE OTHERS ENTER THE TOMB-- TO FIND AN ANGEL SEATED THERE.

DON'T BE FRIGHTENED. JESUS IS RISEN. GO, TELL HIS DISCIPLES.

IN THE CITY PETER AND JOHN ARE SO STARTLED BY MARY'S NEWS THAT THEY RACE BACK AHEAD OF HER. WHEN THEY REACH THE TOMB *

ONLY HIS BURIAL CLOTHES. WHAT DO YOU MAKE OF IT?

THAT HE ROSE FROM THE DEAD-- AS HE SAID HE WOULD. OH, WHY DIDN'T WE BELIEVE HIM!

BY THE TIME MARY REACHES THE GARDEN THE OTHERS HAVE GONE. IN HER GRIEF SHE DOES NOT RECOGNIZE THE VOICE OF ONE WHO QUESTIONS HER.

WHY DO YOU WEEP?

IF YOU HAVE TAKEN JESUS' BODY, TELL ME WHERE YOU HAVE LAID IT.

151

SOFTLY JESUS SPEAKS HER NAME-- "MARY!" SHE TURNS-- AND SEES HER RISEN LORD.

MASTER!

BUT JESUS' FRIENDS ARE NOT THE ONLY ONES WHO ARE EXCITED ABOUT WHAT HAPPENED IN THE GARDEN. IN JERUSALEM THE ROMAN SOLDIERS REPORT TO THE PRIESTS AND PHARISEES. AFRAID OF WHAT MAY HAPPEN IF THE TRUTH IS KNOWN, THEY ACT QUICKLY.

HERE, TAKE THIS MONEY. TELL PEOPLE THAT JESUS' DISCIPLES STOLE HIS BODY.

WHILE THE SOLDIERS SPREAD THEIR LIE, JESUS JOINS TWO OF HIS DISCIPLES ON THE WAY TO EMMAUS. THEY TALK WITH HIM, BUT THEY DO NOT KNOW WHO HE IS.

THAT EVENING AS THEY DINE IN EMMAUS, JESUS BLESSES THE BREAD -- AND WHEN HE HANDS IT TO THEM THEY SUDDENLY RECOGNIZE HIM.

JESUS!

AND JUST AS SUDDENLY HE VANISHES FROM THEIR SIGHT!

OUR BIBLE IN PICTURES

Behind Locked Doors

FROM LUKE 24: 33-43; JOHN 20: 19—21: 6

IT IS LATE SUNDAY NIGHT-- THROUGHOUT JERUSALEM PEOPLE ARE STILL TALKING ABOUT THE STRANGE REPORT OF THE ROMAN SOLDIERS

BUT JESUS' FRIENDS HAVE ALSO HEARD THE SOLDIERS' REPORT. THEY ARE AFRAID THEY MAY BE ARRESTED, SO THEY LOCK THE DOORS IN THE UPPER ROOM WHERE ALL - BUT THOMAS-- HAVE GATHERED. TWO FRIENDS FIND THEM THERE.

154

A WEEK LATER THOMAS IS WITH THE DISCIPLES WHEN THEY MEET AGAIN BEHIND LOCKED DOORS. ONCE MORE JESUS APPEARS TO THEM.

THOMAS, TOUCH MY HANDS AND MY SIDE.

MY LORD AND MY GOD!

BECAUSE YOU HAVE SEEN, THOMAS, YOU BELIEVE. BLESSED ARE THOSE WHO HAVE NOT SEEN AND YET HAVE BELIEVED.

AGAIN JESUS DISAPPEARS FROM THEIR SIGHT.

OBEYING A COMMAND THAT JESUS HAD GIVEN THEM, THE DISCIPLES GO NORTH TO GALILEE. ONE EVENING THEY GO FISHING. THEY FISH ALL NIGHT BUT CATCH NOTHING. AT DAYBREAK THEY SEE THE FIGURE OF A MAN STANDING ON THE SHORE.

CAST YOUR NET ON THE RIGHT SIDE OF THE BOAT.

THEY OBEY—AND SUDDENLY THE NET IS SO FULL OF FISH THEY CANNOT PULL IT IN.

The Last Command

FROM JOHN 21: 7-18; MATTHEW 28: 16-20; LUKE 24: 44-51

ALL NIGHT THE DISCIPLES OF JESUS FISH IN THE SEA OF GALILEE--AND CATCH NOTHING. AT DAYBREAK THEY SEE A MAN ON SHORE WHO TELLS THEM TO CAST THEIR NET ON THE RIGHT SIDE OF THE BOAT. THEY OBEY--AND SUDDENLY THE NET IS SO FULL THAT THE RUGGED FISHERMEN CANNOT DRAW IT UP. JOHN LOOKS AGAIN AT THE FIGURE ON THE SHORE...

LOOK, PETER, IT IS THE LORD!

PETER IS SO EAGER TO REACH JESUS THAT HE JUMPS INTO THE WATER AND SWIMS TO LAND. THE OTHERS BRING THE BOAT IN AND ANCHOR IT OFFSHORE.
AFTER THE NET IS PULLED IN, JESUS CALLS TO HIS HUNGRY DISCIPLES.

COME AND EAT.

FOLLOWING THIS, THE ELEVEN DISCIPLES RETURN TO JERUSALEM. THERE JESUS MEETS WITH THEM AND EXPLAINS HOW--BY HIS DEATH AND RESURRECTION-- HE HAS FULFILLED GOD'S MISSION FOR HIM TO BE THE SAVIOR OF THE WORLD. HE CHARGES THEM TO CARRY ON THE WORK. "BUT WAIT IN JERUSALEM," HE ADDS, "UNTIL THE POWER OF GOD'S HOLY SPIRIT COMES UPON YOU."

ON THE FORTIETH DAY AFTER HIS RESURRECTION, JESUS TAKES HIS DISCIPLES TO THE MOUNT OF OLIVES NEAR BETHANY. AND WHILE HE IS BLESSING THEM, HE ASCENDS INTO HEAVEN.